What You Need to Succeed

Making Car Sales a Career
Rather Than a Job

A Straight Forward, Honest, & Ethical Approach to Selling

by Mike "Radar" Radosevich

Kirk House Publishers
Minneapolis, Minnesota

What You Need to Succeed

Making Car Sales a Career Rather Than a Job

A Straight Forward, Honest, & Ethical Approach to Selling
by Mike "Radar" Radosevich

Library of Congress Cataloging-In-Publication Data

Radosevich, Mike, 1958

What you need to succeed : making car sales a career rather than
a job.

p.cm.

ISBN 1-886513-68-6 (pbd. : alk. paper)

1. Selling--Automobiles. I. Title.

HF5439.A8R33 2003

629.222'068'8--dc22

2003058939

Kirk House Publishers, PO Box 390759, Minneapolis, MN 55439

Manufactured in the United States of America

In Loving Memory

of

Gary Joseph Radosevich

03/31/1936 - 02/26/1999

My Dad...

My Friend...

My Hero!

Contents

Introduction

If you want to be a better salesperson, this is the book for you. If you want to be more successful in your business and personal life, this book is also for you. And if you want to learn the nuts and bolts of selling an automobile, I know this book can really help. But whether it's selling an auto, a boat, or anything else, I've assembled a tried and true formula for being successful.

When I host my two-day seminar on how to professionally sell cars, I always start off the first morning by teaching my students about the importance of attitude management. Then I go on to detail the ten professional steps one needs to accomplish to successfully sell a car. Painful trial and error and 23 years of real-world practice have tested everything I've learned. This sales process is easily adaptable to any product.

I don't think that you thrive in any endeavor unless you've learned to maintain a positive attitude. There are a number of concrete devices I use to keep a positive attitude, and it's that attitude that influences the whole sales process and ultimately makes money and fulfills your goals and dreams. Your inner attitude is the glue that holds the sales process and your life together. Each of the ten steps relates back to the correct attitude and can't be performed if your head is in the wrong place. Each and every day you need to program yourself for success.

Your attitude is fundamental, so I will first deal with attitude management and then dig into the practical sales techniques outlined below.

Ten Steps to a Professional Sale

Step 1   Meet and Greet

Step 2   Interview

Step 3   Select and Demo

Step 4   Feature/Benefit

Step 5   Trade Evaluation

Step 6   Dealership Walk

Step 7   Negotiate and Close/Overcoming Objections

Step 8   Aftermarket and Turn Over

Step 9   Delivery

Step 10 Prospect and Follow-Up

Attitude Management

I believe 90 percent of your success in business and personal life is based on your attitude. I know you've heard that cliché before. But there is nothing, absolutely nothing, I believe more strongly, and I'd like to share with you the manner in which I approach this belief. A lot of us have a hard time keeping our attitudes in the right place because of the negative things that happen around us, many of which are self imposed. In this book I want to concentrate on methods for you to work on the upside of life. It all starts with opening your mind and getting your head in the right place. You must prepare every day for success. On a daily basis you must sincerely embrace the attitudes you need to succeed. I want you to separate yourself from the negative things that ultimately cost you money and happiness. Every day when I get up, I start thinking about what I need to accomplish to reach my goals and ensure my success. You can learn to do the same.

The attitude you embrace on a daily basis is a choice. Success is a decision; it doesn't happen by accident. To embrace a successful attitude you need to decide to make a commitment. The "word" decide, comes from the same root word as homicide, genocide, and suicide. When you "decide" you literally murder your options. If you're going to walk into the car business, or any other business for that matter, and not be truly committed, then you are only cheating yourself. Without giving it a 100 percent commitment you will never succeed to the levels of which you are capable.

Let's talk about society and the meaning of success and failure and how your inner attitude can drive real success in both your business and personal life. The actuaries at big insurance companies can predict just about anything based on a big enough sample of the population. I think it's interesting to look at how society breaks down as a whole when it comes to success. A study was done by the insurance industry using a sample of millions of customers and they came up with the following statistics:

At age 65, out of 100 people:

- One is rich. (He or she is loaded and can do whatever he or she wants.)
- Four are successful. (They are very comfortable and enjoy the good life.)
- Five are still working. (They are probably not so well off if they are still working.)
- 36 are dead.
- 54 are broke.

I conclude from this that 90 percent of us are either dead or dead broke by age 65. Have you ever heard it said that 95 percent of the nation's wealth is controlled by 5 percent of the people? The statistics above are where that saying comes from. Like it or not, everybody reading this is going to end up in one of these categories. Now who decides where you're going to end up? You do, that's who. I believe **"If it is to be, it is up to me."** You have to embrace that kind of attitude about your success.

Were the people in these categories ultimately there because they did make decisions or because they did not?

I understand that as we go through life, we will face challenges and disappointments that we have no control over. These things happen to all of us. It's how one responds to a particular situation that determines success or failure. Was it your fault or was it truly some other condition that you could not control? Your ability to honestly answer that question will determine how long it will take to recover from the challenges and disappointments that life deals you. Do you feel that life has dealt you a bad hand?

Your ability to **accept responsibility for your attitude** is paramount in determining your personal growth and your ability to rebound and recover from negative events in your life. I can't stress that enough. The first step to success is the ability to accept responsibility for your attitude or the results of any shortcomings in your life. The top 5 to10 percent all have this ability.

In a national opinion research study, only 27 percent of those surveyed said they went to work happy and enjoyed what they did. This means that 73 percent are going to work unhappy with what they do for a living. Whose fault is this?

What does this say about our society? Do we live in a negative or a positive world? I think it's negative, and if you need proof, just look at the media. The media is perfect proof of this negativity. Think about it. Take out a newspaper once and cut out every negative article. What have you got left? Car ads!

Seriously, do it once. Watch the news. How many positive reports are there? I don't read newspapers or watch the TV news because it exposes me to negatives. I believe I have a choice to expose myself to either negative or positive influences, and I choose positive. I won't sit in front of the TV news or the newspaper and fill my head with negative and depressing thoughts (There are exceptions like the September 11, 2001 crisis). I know this is a point of disagreement with many people, but it has served me well.

I also don't associate with negative people. When I see the usual coffee clutches at work or salespeople on the showroom floor killing time, I can't help but wonder what everyone is talking about. Is it positive or negative? In most cases they're talking about what's wrong, not what's right.

I have a choice as to whether or not I want to listen. The next time you experience this decision, consider what it costs you in attitude. Sometimes I have come out on the show floor to find a group of four or five salespeople with pitiful and depressed looks on their faces. Misery loves company, and miserable people like to sit together on the pity pot and agree with one another. I'm not saying that you shouldn't have any social time with people at work, but sometimes I have had to say, "Guys, break it up. If a ceiling tile fell, I'd lose a third of my sales staff."

I choose to turn away from that group because I don't need to listen to the "**Mouth of Doom**." "The Mouth of Doom" is a common character in most workplaces. He's on your sales floor, I'll guarantee you that. He has something to gain by getting your attitude down, and believe me, he will cost you money. I refuse to listen to his sermons. I won't expose myself to anything that could potentially cost me money or negatively affect my attitude; the price is just too high. If you let this person rent space in your head, he will eventually own it.

My positive attitude is all-important to me. I take responsibility for it every day. My attitude is directly proportional to my success. We must realize success is not a destination; rather success is a journey itself. Life is a process of becoming; it's certainly not a process of arriving. Anyone that calls success a destination says there is an ending point and in doing so quits growing. There is no end until life itself ends. I love the people who rattle my cage and tug on my brain and make me think about things I never thought about before. Success is a fabulous journey that begins in the moment you are in right now. So what are you going to do about it? If you want it bad enough, you'll get it. If you don't, I don't care because you don't care.

Overcoming the "Thems"

In my long career of selling and managing and as a sales trainer I've had the opportunity to visit countless car dealerships. I like to talk to salespeople and really find out where their heads are. I look at successful people and those who aren't doing so well and try to analyze the difference between the two types. The best explanation I can come up with is that successful people have the ability to accept responsibility for the results. The unsuccessful, on the other hand, always have an excuse.

My conversation with a struggling salesperson usually goes something like this:

"How's it going? How many cars have you sold this month?" I ask.

"Oh, it's kind of slow this month. I only sold eight cars," he mutter?

"How many did you forecast?" I ask.

"Fifteen," he responds.

"Well, what do you think happened? Why are you seven short?" I ask. Now here's where the answer always took on an excuse-ridden response.

"Oh, Radar, you don't understand. The weather's been bad; the factory doesn't have the right programs; the rebates aren't right; I just can't get the right appraisals from my boss; blah, blah, blah..."

This failure is a result of someone or something else, and it's a shame he holds that attitude because there is so much opportunity available if he would just accept responsibility. Sadly, this is the salesperson I see most often. The competition is very weak and the opportunity is great for those who will accept the responsibility.

On the whole, most of us are incapable of accepting responsibility for our failures. We want to blame failures on "them." I always ask, who are the "thems" of your life? What outside negative influences have kept you from success? Who are the people you can bum it off on to hold yourself in place and give yourself whatever excuses you need to stay the way you are, to avoid changing and becoming something better? Is it possible that by changing your inner attitudes, you can change your outer circumstances? People with a "them" attitude have come to the conclusion that they are victims of their circumstances rather than creators of them. They have adopted a victim's mentality.

Know Your Industry and Your Competition

Let me share with you some statistics from the National Automobile Dealers Association, NADA, to help you understand the great opportunity you have to be successful in the automobile industry. These numbers will help you compare yourself and your dealership to your competition in an industry where billions of dollars are spent to sell millions of cars.

NADA said last year (2001) that its new car dealer body in the U.S. consisted of 21,400 car dealerships. Those dealerships sold about 17.1 million vehicles and spent billions of dollars in advertising. Yes, that's billions just on new cars. Now of course there are also used car dealers, almost 40,000. These dealers also sold millions of used cars last year.

There are over 60,000 car dealerships in the U.S. That's a beautiful number to me. I wake up every morning knowing one thing: I will never be unemployed unless it's my own choice. I have more job security than anyone I know. If you're successful in this business, you'll get job offers left and right. What are dealerships typically looking for? Experience. They don't want to put up with the frustrations of training "green peas" and those with limited sales experience. So I just love the number 60,000, and I hope you come to a point in your career when you do too.

Advertising Fuels Sales

On top of the billions of dollars in advertising spent by car dealerships, foreign and domestic manufacturers also spent billions on new car ads. It all adds up to the biggest advertising budget on earth spent last year to do just one thing: **get people on the show floor to give you an opportunity to succeed**.

How are these billions in high-octane advertising brought to us? Through TV, radio, newspapers, magazines, print, outdoor, direct mail, and the Internet. Think of all the times you're exposed to a message from a manufacturer or car dealer. The National Advertising Council estimates the average American is exposed to 30,000 commercials per year—one third of those commercials is car ads. That means the average American is exposed to over 20 car messages per day. I know that seems like a lot, but watch a football game or your favorite TV shows and count them. Test it. The repetition of all these commercials entices the buyer to visit a dealership. Basically, advertising creates the desire, paving the way for you to have the opportunity to make the sale.

You Make the Difference

When a customer or a potential customer sets out to look at vehicles, what is this person really shopping for? I believe this customer is shopping for a salesperson more than he or she is shopping for a vehicle. As I said, your competition is very weak. To prove that point, let me give you some follow-up customer sales survey figures provided by Sales Support Inc., a company that specializes in the auto industry.

- Prospects who bought within three days: 57 percent
- Prospects who bought within a week: 77 percent
- Closing ratio for first time prospects (first time "ups"—prospects who walk in): 19 percent
- Closing ratio on "be-back" prospects: 54 percent (That's 2.5 times the closing ratio if you get them back in the dealership.)
- Closing ratio on referrals: 57 percent
- Closing ratio on repeat customers: 67 percent

This is why I focus so much on ongoing contact with your entire customer base. The following survey results should help you see why this is so valuable to your success in this business.

- Prospects who were not followed up with after leaving the dealership — 90%
- Owners who were not contacted by the salesperson after delivery regarding the purchase of another vehicle:" 90 percent.
- Customers who did not recall the salesperson's name 12 months after delivery: 82 percent
- The number one reason a customer bought where they did wasn't the location, wasn't the product, wasn't the price—it was the salesperson.

Now, that's pretty weak competition, and that should give you some confidence. To be perfectly honest with you, I hope those numbers do not change. I always felt it gave me the opportunity to stand apart from my competition.

Let's face it—upon returning from shopping for a car, most people recount nothing but bad experiences and frustration. What do they say when they are at the lunch table at work or with their friends and the topic of conversation turns to car buying? "Horrible." "Degrading." "Worse than a root canal."

I know what they say, and I did everything I could to change the stereotype. I had customers who said, "It's not that way with Radar." I got hundreds of referrals from satisfied customers who had positive experiences with me. I made a commitment to treat every customer in a professional manner, with respect, honesty, and dignity. Just like I would want to be treated if I were buying a car.

Take the "Up". . . Recognize Their Interest

When a potential customer walks onto a lot, I hear lot of salespeople say, "Oh, they're just kicking tires" or "I'm tired of these people that aren't serious about buying a car." They hang back and ignore the potential customer. They won't approach the customer and take what we in the car industry call an "up," which is an opportunity to make a sale.

I guess I never embraced that attitude. Because what does their presence on the lot tell me? It says they are here because they have some level of interest. I always went after every "up" with a 100 percent selling effort, regardless of how serious I thought they were. I did this because I can't tell you how many cars I've sold in my life where the customer said, "Radar, we weren't even looking at buying a car today."

What happened in those cases was that I gave the customers the information they needed to make the decision to purchase. That's probably the highest compliment any customer can give you. They came in with a limited amount of interest and in the end made the decision to buy.

Why do some people trade for a new car every year or two? Are there people who do that? Of course there are, but why? Maybe they don't want to risk mechanical, failure, or maybe they need a different vehicle because of life changes.

But what really happens is that new models come out every year. The car manufacturers change features constantly in an effort to entice us to come in and buy the new creature comforts or have the new body style. The bottom line is that a combination of repetitive advertising and the creation of new features and models create a desire in the customer's mind. It works! Otherwise the manufacturers and dealers would not be spending this kind of money on advertising and development. With all this working for you, you should be eager to take every "up" that comes your way. If you do you'll increase your chances for success.

So now that we've established what a powerful interest there is in cars and their features—why do some salespeople fail so often? One of their big flaws is that they prejudge people.

We're all guilty of prejudging people. We prejudge their ability or intent to buy by the way they look, what they currently drive, or the way they are dressed or groomed. I get a kick out of salespeople who look out the window and see someone on the lot and say, "Oh they're just kicking tires." Well, if you can possibly qualify someone's ability to buy from 50 yards away, I'm going to set you up with Dionne Warwick's "Psychic Friends Network," because that's where you belong.

Some of the poorest looking people I've ever seen in my life paid cash for their cars. Maybe you have already experienced this situation. So don't prejudge; everyone deserves your respect.

Let me tell you about another character I've seen a lot in the car business. I call him "Joe-Bag-A-Donuts." This is the guy who is sitting at his desk with his feet up, donut in one hand and sports page in the other. Maybe there's a stain on his shirt and crumbs on his desk. When a customer walks in Joe barely looks up from the sports page and barks, "Can I help you?"

"Yes," the customer meekly responds, "I'm interested in looking at some cars."

Joe, in-between bites of his donut, doesn't miss a beat. He says, "Well the new cars are here and the used cars over there. If you see something you like, let me know and I'll get you a good deal."

That's how a good share of your competition approaches a prospect, and how little work they put into it. There's a total lack of sales effort.

I drive 50,000 miles a year. I need dependability and don't want to risk mechanical failure, so I tend to trade more often than most people. I prefer to buy from one of my clients, but sometimes I can't find exactly what I'm looking for, so it causes me to shop other dealerships.

I drive my Lexus onto the dealership lot. I'm dressed nicely, usually in a suit and tie. Now, if I don't look like I could potentially afford to buy a car, then I guess I don't know who does. There are a lot of times I have to go up and ask for help. Salespeople are standing inside the door, watching me walk the lot, and I don't get waited on. Or, I get waited on and within the first two minutes the salesperson asks, "Are you here to buy a car today or are you just looking?" I swear to God that's how poor the sales effort often is.

There's a very chauvinistic attitude held by some salespeople when it comes to women buyers. Many bright, well-educated, and successful women who shop for cars on their own report being patronized by unenlightened salespeople who underestimate their abilities. Selling to women is an important factor in your success, because I've heard that over 80 percent of the cars sold last year involved the decision of a woman. If you have chauvinistic attitudes you'd better lose them pretty quickly because if your customer feels that you don't appreciate the fact that she can make her own decisions, she's going to throw you under the bus so far that you're never going to get out.

I see this chauvinistic attitude when I send salespeople out shopping. I will send a woman from one of my classes shopping alone and then tell her to bring along a man to a second dealership. It's very common for the male salesperson to focus his sales effort on the guy even though the car is for the woman. Big mistake!

Back to "Joe-Bag-A-Donuts" for a minute. He's the guy who puts forth the minimum sales effort. He's an order taker, not a salesperson. Last year, the average salesperson in the car business sold between 8 and 10 cars a month. One of the biggest problems in the car business is there are too many people that are comfortable at $3,000 to $3,500 per month. They don't aspire to be any better; they don't have to be any better. They are selling enough cars to keep their jobs and don't feel the need to challenge themselves and take the responsibility to change. It's a problem!

Now a lot of you might be happy with that level of pay. I understand it might sound like good money to some of you depending on what you have been paid in your life. But I'm here to tell you there are an awful lot of people in this business who do much better than that. They are the ones who embrace long term attitudes and philosophies about this business that ultimately result in a six-figure income. I'm not talking about managers; I'm talking about salespeople. Aspire to be better than average.

Activity Level

Beginning this moment, concentrate on your activity level. It has a lot to do with your attitude and your success. If you go to work and are busy all day long, even if you didn't make a sale, you come home with a positive attitude. You felt you were productive, that you planted seeds for the future. You wake up the next morning and you say to yourself, "Man, I worked hard yesterday, I took three ups, I did all my follow-up calls. I studied my product and generally did all the things I needed to ensure my success in this business." When you head out the door for work in the morning, you're happy to be going. You are one of the select 27 percent who likes to go to work.

Now, let's say it's slow on customer traffic at the dealership and you decide not to do anything; not school yourself or do follow up, or plant any seeds. You go home with the blahs. When you wake up the next morning, what's your attitude like? You probably say, "Oh man, I got to get up and go through that again? What a drudge!"

You have to see that **your positive attitude will be in direct proportion to your activity level.** And furthermore, your income will be in direct proportion to your attitude.

When you're in a good mood, it's infectious. When's the best time to sell a car? After you just sold one, when your head's in the right place. But if your dobber's down, you're doing that customer, yourself, and the dealership a

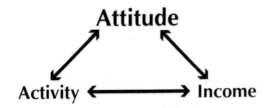

It all starts with attitude!

terrible disservice. You have to get your head in the right place. At times, we all need a *"check up from the neck up."* We have to flush out our heads and find a way to overcome it.

It all starts with activity level. Your attitude is in direct proportion to your activity level and your income is in direct proportion to your attitude. I can't repeat that enough!

I know salespeople who set themselves up for failure by mentally spending the sales commission before the vehicle is delivered. Say you write a deal and there's a $500 commission. The next day the deal falls out of bed because you can't get it financed, or the people change their minds, or some third baseman gets involved and mucks it up. What happens? The salesperson goes into a tailspin for a week and can't sell a car because all they can think about is what they've lost—what somebody else did to them.

If I can give you a good piece of advice, don't mentally spend a commission until the car is delivered. I mean bustin' bugs, tail-lights across the curb and delivered. That's the only time you've really earned it. Yes, you have the potential of making it, but it won't crush you if you don't spend the commission in your mind before you have the right to.

The people I talk about who have the "thems" in their lives ultimately end up having a lot more lows than highs. We're all good at one thing, and that's letting ourselves off the hook. Aren't we? When I talk about goals I'll illustrate that point even more clearly.

Negativity and Overcoming Fear

Let's talk more about living in a negative society and also about the difference between success and failure and how we got to the point where 73 percent of us aren't happy going to work each morning. How have we become such a negative society? I've told you why I don't read a newspaper or watch the TV news. But you have to ask yourself, how sick have we become as a society when that's all we'll buy? Realize this: if we wouldn't buy it, they wouldn't sell it, right? If we wouldn't watch it or read it, then they wouldn't keep shoveling it at us. There are enough negatives already. I don't need to invite more into my life or brain. How did we get to a point where we have such a terrible amount of fear?

Why do we have so much fear?

Look at the 73 percent that are unhappy going to work. Why do they continue to work at the same job if they are not happy? The answer is that they are afraid of failure and change.

When I think of how we have become laden with fear as people, both the fear of change and fear of living in a negative world, I think of the human brain. The fastest computer in the world is your brain. Your brain can process about 100,000 pieces of information per second. Keep in mind that all the opinions we embrace are a result of previous experiences.

First off, we use just 10 percent to 15 percent of our brains. There are certain things that happen in our lives that go below conscious recognition that make impressions on our brain and that make us develop certain attitudes and philosophies about life. If I told you to raise your right hand and you raised it, you'd be making a conscious decision. But if told to stop your heart, you couldn't. Certain events enter our brains beneath our conscious recognition and we don't notice their impact. Ultimately these experiences make impressions in our brain and form the attitudes and opinions that we embrace.

How is all this information brought to our brain? Through our senses of sight, sound, smell, taste, and touch. The most important is hearing, and what's the message most people hear from an early age? Let me take you to Anytown, USA, Friday at 5:00 p.m. Mr. & Mrs. "Joe-Bag-A-Donuts" are sitting around the supper table with five year-old little Joey, and what's the main topic of conversation? "Thank God it's Friday." "Life's a drag." So on and so forth . . . that's what this kid is being exposed to at an early age.

Freud said the age of reasoning is seven years old, and prior to the age of seven the average child is exposed to one word more than any other. You guessed it, that word is **"NO!"** Kids are pretty fearless and resilient but as we grow older, what one word do we try to avoid the most? It's **"NO!"** That's where all the fear is. Understand that fear is reduced or eliminated with confidence. Confidence is built through knowledge.

Here's a good example to illustrate this point. If I take a sturdy board and set it on my living room floor and bet you $10 you can't walk across without falling off, I'm sure you'll take that bet. Then, if I bet you $20 you can't walk across the same board if I spread it across two tables in my kitchen, I'm sure you'll take that bet. Now, what would you think if I bet you $1000 and took that same board and ran it from a windowsill on the12th floor of a hotel to the windowsill on the 12th floor of a bank? Now you're thinking, "Not even for a $1,000, I won't do it." You're thinking, "That's my blood down there!"

The inner balance of your ear hasn't changed. Your sense of balance has remained unaltered. The board is the same. A task you successfully performed twice before you're now incapable of doing not because of any change of task, but because of a change of *attitude*. Standing on top of the hotel, you're projecting yourself toward what you *don't* want rather than toward what you *do* want. Concentrating on the negative holds you in place. You're stuck.

I've often thought we spend too much time thinking about the sales we've lost than the sales we've made and the ones we are going to make.

Let's change the board-walking scenario one more time. You're in the bank building and the hotel is burning and one of your kids is in the burning hotel. Now what do you do? You don't even hesitate, do you? You'll walk on the board if your child is at risk. So what really controls our decision-making power? Fear is what controls more of our decisions than any other factor.

We all want to protect our ego and stay where it's comfortable. Your ego controls your decision-making. Think back to high school and the pretty girl you wanted ask to the dance, but didn't. Why was that? The answer is simple: you feared the word "NO!" "Good job, you protected me," says your ego. You can stay comfortable.

That fear of hearing no will prevent you from succeeding in this or any other business. Why? Because we have to ask people to buy or we can't make the sale. I hear from sales managers all the time who say that the salesperson does a great job but won't pull the trigger and ask someone to buy. That comes from the fear of hearing no. We often work hard getting to the point that we're convinced we've earned the right to ask the customer to buy then come up short because of our fears.

If you are thorough enough in the first six steps of selling, which we'll talk about shortly, then you've earned the right to ask the customer to buy. Believe that. I've never had a problem asking for the sale because of that. I always felt I'd rolled out the red carpet for the customer and had earned the right to ask them to buy.

Goal Setting

I've never grown when I was comfortable, and I try to take myself outside my comfort zone in a lot of different areas. If I look honestly at my weaknesses and deal with things with which I'm uncomfortable, then I become a much more rounded person and more capable of overcoming the obstacles that life puts in front of me. I encourage you to take yourself out of your comfort zone and try to grow as a person. Goal setting is the best way to do this.

Who has goals in their lives? Everybody has goals, but do any of you have them written down? I believe that **"An unwritten goal is nothing more than a wish."** To make your goals a reality you must first write them down. Here's the method I use to ensure my success. First, I write the words **"MY GOALS"** on top of a blank sheet of paper. Play along and try doing this for yourself. Think back three years ago from today, then write that date down and ask these questions:

a. Where did you live?

b. What did you drive?

c. How much money did you make annually?

d. How much money was in savings and investments?

e. Where did you go on vacation?

f. On a scale of one to ten, ten being the highest, rate your overall happiness, both personally and professionally?

Then do the same exercise for right now, whatever the current year is. Answer the same questions. Then let's think about where you want to be three years from now. To set realistic goals you need to think about where you have been, where you are now, and where you'd like to be. Basically, if we want to know where we're going, we need to know where we've been.

Try it! Make a chart that looks something like this:

MY GOALS

Questions:	3 Yrs Ago	Today	In 3 Years
Where did you live?			
What did you drive?			
How much $ did you make annually?			
How much $ in savings and investments?			
Where did you go on vacation?			
Rate your happiness on a scale of 1-10			

Your goals need to be realistic. Don't set yourself up for failure. I will adjust my long term goals over the course of time if I see I'm ahead of schedule, or if I feel I can just push the edge of the envelope and find out what I'm really worth in a particular area. Make them realistic, but challenge yourself and write them down, because **"An unwritten goal is nothing more than a wish."**

Take a look at what has happened over the past three years. If it was not what you wanted to happen, then you need to find the reasons why you fell short. Did you set your goals too high? Are you blaming the "thems" in your life for keeping you away from your dreams? Did you lack inspiration, or drive? Be honest and look deep into yourself.

What's your motivation?

Why strive for success in the first place you might ask? Is it worth it?

To answer that, I believe everyone needs to find his own personal inspiration. I've found the most effective way to accomplish my goals is to find my own personal inspiration. I believe that you will **do for someone else what you will not do for yourself.** My personal inspiration is my wife and kids. I do it for them. I make commitments to them and revolve my goals around fulfilling those commitments.

One example is my daughter Angie. Her grades came down from her previous accomplishments when she was a 15-year-old freshman in high school. She was not doing what she was capable of doing. I asked, "Angie, what do you want for your 16th birthday next year?" We all know the answer to that one, don't we? She wanted wheels—a car. So I made a deal with her. If she could bring her grades back up to a 3.5 grade point average, then I would buy her a car for her 16th birthday. She worked hard that whole year. Her grades came up and she brought home a 3.67 GPA on her 16th birthday. I gave her the Acura Legend I was driving. She had a goal. I put it in front of her. She gobbled it right up. So, it works. I don't do it for me—I do it for them! As my sons Michael and Tyler have gotten older, I've done the same.

By making that commitment to them, now I'm doing it for them. Here's what's neat about it: if I don't meet my goals and keep my end of the bargain, but my kids keep their end of the deal and remain good students, then how would I feel about myself? That would be a tough one. My commitments drive me everyday. I make commitments to them—to my wife and children.

You have to find your own personal inspiration; it might be your wife, husband, or significant other, a boyfriend, girlfriend, or God and family. The point is **do it for someone else and you'll get there more often.**

Last thing you need to do is establish a plan of attack. In other words, what do you need to do on a daily, weekly, and monthly basis to ensure your success? Some of you can't do this exercise now, because you don't know what you need to do in this business to ensure you reach those goals. But after you read this book you'll have the ammunition to succeed.

I'll teach you how to evaluate yourself honestly and you'll know what course of action is needed for you to become as effective as you possibly can be in this business. We all have weaknesses. I know I've got them, and you've got them too, but until we identify them in a cool and clinical manner we have no way of knowing what needs correction or what to accept responsibility for. If you can approach this task honestly, I know you can get there.

I have my goals plastered all over the place. I make copies of them. I try to wake up every morning with my goals right in front of me. There were times when I had them taped to the bathroom mirror. When I was getting ready for work, my goals were the first thing on my mind. You see, I'm programming myself for success by doing this. I'll put them in my office, my car, and my wallet. I can't get away from them. This technique increases your focus to get wherever you want to be. Let's face it, we all have different aspirations. How high can you jump, how far can you leap? None of us really knows. Nobody can put a price tag on you but you. Nobody preordained that you're a $50,000 a year man or $100,000 a year woman. How much can you accomplish? I don't know, you don't know, none of us know how many cars we can possibly sell or what else we can achieve.

The other thing I believe in doing on a monthly basis is to set a base, an acceptable bottom. Not only should you detail how far ahead you want to get, but also regardless of what happens, you need a limit to how low you'll accept. It's your excuse level. Say to yourself, "I am not going below 10 cars no matter what happens, and if I do, it's 100% my fault." That's where your head needs to be. Initially, it's more important to put out an acceptable base than how high you want to go. If you do that, you'll find a lot of success and you'll wind up going beyond those levels a lot faster.

Manage Your Goals

Break your sales goals down to something shorter than a month. I know so many salespeople who set a goal to sell 15 cars a month but never figure out, based on their closing percentage, how many ups they have to take or what their activity level needs to be. They get to the 27th of the month with ten cars sold and are scrambling to meet their goal. The fact of the matter is that they basically took the first ten days off. They didn't take three ups a day like they ought to. Every single day I knew where I was. If I wanted to sell 20 cars a month, I needed to take 50 ups. Now, 50 contacts in the dealership per month, divided by 23 working days, is a little more than two ups a day. If you are new in the business, I'm going to teach you to take three ups a day initially, because as a beginner you probably won't close above 30 percent.

If I got to the third day of the month and only had four ups, instead of six, then I knew I had to find two more ups to keep on track. You don't eat an elephant in one bite. You swallow it daily, weekly, and monthly.

When I got to work in the morning the first thing I did was write down some goals. For instance:

1. Take three *ups* today.
2. Study product knowledge for an hour focusing on my weaknesses.
3. Practice sales *Steps 2 and 3* because I'm losing customers there.
4. Make ten prospect calls.

5. Call past customers as detailed in *Step 10*.

Typically, after three or four months selling cars, the thing people dislike the most is the down time in the business. Those times when you just don't know what to do have a tendency to bring your attitude down. Instead of keeping their activity level up along with their attitudes, many salespeople get trapped into negative thinking and do nothing. If they drive down that road for long, they'll come to the conclusion they are the victims of their circumstances rather than creators of them. They forget that their attitude is in direct proportion to their activity level and their income level is in direct proportion to their attitude.

If you continue to read this whole book with a sincere and honest effort, I'll arm you with enough to do that you'll never get bored. If you commit to doing all the things I'll explain in the chapters ahead, you will develop a passion for success. Remember, **"Life without passion is a pretty shallow existence."**

Things to remember:

- Choose to succeed and give it 100 percent commitment.
- Choose to be positive and avoid negative influences.
- Take and accept responsibility.
- Treat every customer in a professional manner, with respect, honesty and dignity.
- Take every "up" that comes your way and approach it with an open mind.
- Get rid of chauvinistic attitudes.
- Your positive attitude will be in direct proportion to your activity level.
- Your income will be in direct proportion to your attitude.
- Conduct a checkup from the neck up.
- Overcome your fears.
- Take yourself outside your comfort zone.
- Set goals and write them down.
- Find your personal inspiration.
- Manage your goals.

Meet and Greet

Goals:

- Make a positive first impression.
- Give the customer a "different experience."
- Increase the customer's comfort level.

With each step there will be goals you want to accomplish within the body of that step. Meet and greet is the first step in the sales process, and here's how you do it.

First impressions are very important because you only get one chance to make a good first impression. You want to smile and look the customers in the eye. For anybody that feels the need to wear sunglasses, I hope you'll reconsider that. If I can't see someone's eyes, I have a real problem believing what they are trying to tell me. I've had salespeople say they had sensitive eyes. That may be so, but I don't know how you can build trust and avoid eye contact at the same time.

Your attire should be neat and consistent with your dealership dress code. You should be well groomed and professional in appearance.

Personal space is very important. You probably know people in your lives that need to be too close to you when they talk. I'm really uncomfortable when someone gets six or eight inches from my face during conversation. We've all got a certain amount of personal space we need in order to feel comfortable. Four to six feet is a good rule. The only time I'll invade that personal space is upon handshake.

No pouncing! Some of you are aggressive people, I understand, but keep in mind we are trying to bring these people closer and closer to us, not push them away. And when salespeople are over aggressive, customers have a tendency to back away.

I also want to give the customer a **"different experience."** I think it's important to discover what's going on in a customer's head when they come out and look for a car. First of all, are they looking forward to it? In most cases they are not. The reason they don't like shopping for a car is because of past experiences. They've got fear, and their number one fear is paying too much. That's not what you want to talk about in the early steps. They come in with a protective bubble around them, and it's your job, as a professional to slowly dissolve that bubble, not burst it. Take their wall down one brick at a time, one step at a time and really try to bring them closer to you. Do that by asking open-ended, non-threatening, non-confrontational questions and continue that process through all the sales steps. You have to give a "different experience" than your competition and set yourself apart if you want to make a positive first impression.

What's the most common way of greeting a customer when they enter a store? What do most people say? They say, **"Can I help you?"** Think about that for a second. What's your immediate knee-jerk reaction when asked, "Can I help you?"

The usual response is **"I'm just looking."** That's an objection, and it's the last thing you want to hear. If you use that greeting you're actually inviting an objection, one that's extremely hard to overcome. You have only two choices if a customer says, "I'm just looking." One is to hover over them and potentially make them even more uncomfortable. The other is to hand them a business card and say you'll check back later. Neither advances the sales process.

Throughout the steps, the word tracks you use are going to help you keep the ball rolling and move you to the next step. If you're hearing, "I'm just looking" too often, then you should take a look at the way you are greeting. The definition of insanity is doing the same thing over and over again and expecting different results. Keep on doing what you've always done and you'll keep on getting what you've always gotten. If you can't get past step one you need to change your approach. You'll never get to step two, and of course you'll never get to step seven, which is the ultimate goal.

So, how can you avoid hearing "I'm just looking?"

First, you need a salutation. You might say "hello," "hi," or "howdy"— whatever fits your personality. Next, I always like to begin with small talk. I don't believe in jumping right into the sales process and would rather start with something other than cars. Keep in mind there is tension and customers are afraid to make a mistake. They've had bad experiences and you want to give them a different, more positive feeling. You want to break the ice and make them feel comfortable. Your goal at this point is to increase their comfort level and reduce their fears.

Talk about the weather and say, "Boy, what a beautiful day to be out looking for a car." They might have a Vikings' or a Packers' starter jacket on and you could say, "How about those Vikes this year?" Talk about something other than the car deal. I always keep my eyes open to spot a bumper sticker or things in their car that might give me a clue about a hobby or interest. If I saw hunting gear for instance I might mention it because I like to hunt, fish, and golf, and I enjoy talking about those activities. You need to find common ground throughout the sales process and initial small talk is a good place to start. Get into small talk first!

Then when it feels right say, "By the way, welcome to ____(your dealership)__. My name is ___(use your full name)___. And yours?" At this time begin your handshake.

Let's discuss the handshake for a moment. Is a handshake important? Does your handshake affect the way someone might perceive you? Yes, a handshake is important. Have you ever gotten a weak, limp handshake? Were you impressed by it? No. A handshake needs to be firm but not overpowering and your hand needs to be in all the way.

Is it different for a man or a woman? Whose hand should you shake first if a man and woman come in together? If you have to walk around the guy to get to the woman, he might not like that. I always went to the one that was closest to me and if they were the same distance from me it really didn't matter. As I'm shaking their hand I say, **"Hi, my name is Mike Radosevich; my friends and customers call me Radar. And your name is?"**

After the handshake, what happens 30 seconds after you meet someone? You forget their name don't you? We all do it. You do it because you're thinking about where you are going in the conversation and not where you are at the moment. How can we make sure we don't forget their names? We write them down, that's how. I always carry a little note pad in my shirt or pant pocket. I just say to the customer, **"If you don't mind, I think I'll just jot that down so I don't forget it."** You can phrase this in a way that's comfortable for you, but try writing the word track down and practicing it. Customers can certainly identify with this request because we all forget names when we meet new people. The most embarrassing thing that can happen is that you get to the third step of the sale and have to ask, "What was your name again?"

After the handshake, to make sure they don't forget my name I say, "Let me give you one of my business cards." Most salespeople don't give business cards out until the end, which is too late. I believe in getting the introductions out of the way in the beginning, and using both first and last names. When I volunteer my full name to a customer, he or she is more comfortable giving me their full name. First, it shows the customer that you care about their name and second, you don't want to forget it because you'll need it to follow-up the customer if they leave the dealership without buying. I also like to justify everything I do with a customer. You don't want to get to step three without the customer or salesperson knowing the other's name. That's unprofessional!

For many of the sales steps, like the "meet and greet" sequence above, I'll be suggesting word tracks that will improve your sales success. Initially, you'll want to learn them word for word. Learning scripted material is much easier than trying to fly by the seat of your pants. You may sound wooden at first, but it's no different than hearing a new song on the radio. After four or five times you suddenly know all the words.

I might say it differently than you do. I understand I can't be you and you can't be me; however, you'll eventually make the words your own, and you'll sound very natural. I learn to recall a lot of things, presentations in particular, by putting my own voice on tape and listening to it over and over again. There are 18 questions in step two, and you need to get them all committed to memory. The only way you can do that is by studying. Write your script and practice it. You need to know the word tracks and where you are at all times in the sales process. If you know what step you are on and what steps are next, you can succeed.

The sales process is like a rolling ball: it starts at step one and should roll along step after step. I want to keep that ball rolling forward. We often make little mistakes that send the ball backwards or stop it, and that's what we want to try to avoid. You really need to prepare yourself and learn all the steps. In other words, when we get further along in the sales process you'll see how it all comes together and how each step is an important part of the whole deal. A number of things that I suggest may seem trite and insignificant right now. In the end, you'll understand why they're so vital to your success.

Things to remember:

- Eye to eye contact.
- Personal space 4-6 feet.
- Attire and grooming.
- No sunglasses.
- No pouncing.
- Avoid "Can I help you?"—"No, just looking."
- Scripting word tracks and practicing until they are natural.
- Start with small talk.
- Handshake, introduction with full name, present business card.
- "If you don't mind, I think I'll just jot that down so I don't forget it."

Interview

Goals:

- Identify wants and needs.
- Build rapport, find common ground, and be a good listener.
- Ask non-threatening, non-confrontational, open-ended questions.
- Identify "Hot Buttons" and dominant buying motive.

Interview is the qualifying portion of the sales process. In this step you'll learn 18 questions, the answers of which will help you identify wants, needs, and "hot buttons," and determine the customer's "dominant buying motive."

Throughout the qualifying portion you want to ask non-confrontational, non-threatening, open-ended questions. By an open-ended question I mean a question that must be answered by something other than a yes or a no.

There are three phases to the Interview process: Product, Personal, and Trade. Within each of these phases you will ask precise questions to lay the ground-work for the rest of the sale and enable you to find common ground and build rapport.

"Have you spoken with any of our salespeople previously?"

After presenting a business card you should be sure to ask this question. I wish every store had a policy to ask that question; there would be fewer conflicts between salespeople and more harmony at the dealership.

If I am dealing with someone else's customer I'd like to know it up front. If the customer answers yes, I'll offer to get that salesperson for them because I want to stay clean with my coworkers. On the other hand, the customer may say, yeah, I talked with some Jim guy last week but I don't want to talk with him now. In that case, I'll help the customer myself. At that point I can tell my manager that I knew it was Jim's customer and he or she didn't want to deal with Jim. Perhaps something went wrong between them—let's face it, some personalities just don't click. It would be great if we could match the customer's personality to the right salesperson. You need to ask this question up front because you don't want the hassle of fighting over commissions with your coworkers.

Identify the right vehicle:
Are you interested in a new or used vehicle?

I need to expand on this a little bit. Some stores use what they call an 'open show floor' which means every salesperson takes both new and used car *ups*. Other dealerships have a 'closed show floor,' where some salespeople sell new cars and others sell used, and you can't cross territories unless you have a repeat, a referral, or possibly a customer who started in one department but changed their mind.

If they are interested in a used car and you're a new car salesperson, you should walk them to the used car department. You shouldn't just say used cars are over there. Most people are going to do that—point the customers in the direction and let them go on their own. I used to send them to the salespeople I endorsed in the used car building. That approach resulted in many of those salespeople returning the favor to me and also shows the rest of the staff that you're not taking a used car *up* when you're not a used car salesperson. I just tried to stay as clean as I could with all the other salespeople. It's the right thing to do.

Are you familiar with our product line?

Customers usually reply yes to this question and you should respond by saying, **"Great, which model did you come to see today?"**

We are in the age of consumerism, and customers have a lot of product knowledge. They pull facts off the Internet or read brochures and magazines like *Road and Track, Car and Driver,* or *Consumer Reports.* Today's buyer is the most informed and educated ever. They read the advertising and are versed in price and payment. The bottom line is that they come to shop one or two models. Sometimes they say, "Well, I'm not sure I can afford a Grand Am. I want to look at that, but I might have to go with a Sunfire." Or maybe they'll say, " I want to look at an Accord if I can afford it, but I might have to consider a Civic."

If, and only if, the customer admits that they've been shopping, ask them "What other vehicles are you considering?" Learn about your competition. What advantages does your product have over your competitions?

In What body style are you interested?

When the customer tells you which model he or she likes, you should inquire further and ask about the body style he or she prefers. For instance, if the customer said Grand Am, ask if he wants a two-door or a four-door model. Some cars come in two-door, four-door, and wagon models. Customers may say they want to look at a pick-up. OK, do you want regular cab or extended cab, 2-wheel drive, or four-wheel drive, number of doors, long bed, regular bed, etc.? It's imperative that you know your product so you can find out what customers really want and what's available.

What basic equipment do you need on your new car?

Why start with basic equipment? Salespeople lose car deals on a daily basis, lots of them, because they start the customer out with too much vehicle.

People who normally want simple features like tilt, cruise, air, or automatic, will eventually inquire about more luxurious creature comforts when it comes time. By starting with a basic model you have the opportunity to plant seeds about positive features that are available and justify the value of those features.

For example, if the customer wants basic features like tilt, cruise, air, power windows and power door locks, and you're looking at a Honda Accord, bring them to a basic Accord LX 4-cylinder, don't start with a loaded EX 6-cylinder with leather. Even though some of us have a tendency to sell up, it's better to get the customer sold on the basic LX first. If customers are comfortable with the basic model, it's an easier step for them to spend $1500 to $2500 more for the next package, and it's their own choice. Most importantly, if they are sold on the value of the basic car it's easier for them to recognize and appreci-ate the value of added features.

If I do this in reverse, however, starting them out with too much car, then eventually I've got to subtract something and bring their ego down a notch. The last thing a customer wants to say is, "No, I can't afford that!"

Have you ever thought about the difference between wants and needs? Would you rather have a customer that wants a car or needs a car? I'd rather have a customer that wants a car, because then it's an emotional decision. When I started selling clothes at age 16, I ultimately developed a passion for selling and I wanted to know all I could about it. I started studying the subject back in the days when the common sales philosophy was "finding a need and filling it." That attitude has changed over the years. Let's be clear—people don't need a $30,000 vehicle. Getting from point A to point B can be fulfilled with a $100 car. As salespeople, if we were just fulfilling needs, we would just be clerking. The ability to create a want where no need exists is now the role of a professional salesperson. Wanting is emotional; needing is rational.

Do you prefer a light, medium, or dark color?

Why would I ask it that way rather than ask what color they want? First of all, I don't want to get them locked down on a color I might not have in stock. Sell what you see; don't see what you can sell. You can't deliver a car today that isn't in stock. Yes, a dealer trade or special order is possible and some people are absolutely set on a color. They want bright red—period. You don't want to be too specific on color. See if they are flexible. Also, most customers don't know every color that the car comes in. While on an inventory walk with you, a customer might be attracted to a color he or she didn't even know was available.

Great, come with me!

It's not an open-ended question, but once you've gone this far you've earned the right to be a little assertive. Notice I didn't ask, "Do you want to come with me?" Instead I directed and said, "Great, come with me." You also have to show your ability to take control of the situation, and sometimes it's appropriate to do so. There are more sheep than shepherds in this world, and we've been conditioned our entire life to do as we're told. As kids our parents and teachers say, "Do as you're told." You go to work, and your boss says, "Do as you're told." You get married and your spouse says, "Do as you're told." We are used to it. Use statements like, "Come with me." "Have a seat." "Sign here." There are a few points during the sales steps where assertiveness is helpful and appropriate, but you have to earn it.

What are the three most important things to you in the purchase of your next vehicle?

This last product question is one I've never been asked while buying anything. You should ask it to every single customer, no matter what you're selling, because this is where you'll find the customer's "hot buttons" and "dominant buying motives."

The problem with most salespeople is that they don't really listen to the customer's desires and launch into the same sales presentation for every customer. They do minimal qualifying and proceed to steps three and four, *Select and Demo* and *Feature and Benefit,* without having the information to tailor a presentation for that specific customer. Every customer has different wants and needs, hot buttons, and dominant buying motives, and each deserves to be treated as a unique and valued individual.

If I asked each of you what were the three most important things to you in the purchase of a vehicle, there would be a wide array of answers. They could be color, price, payments, anti-lock brakes, suspension, safety, gas mileage, power, comfort, etc.

I'm not going to give a performance presentation on suspensions and horsepower when the customer is primarily interested in gas mileage and safety. How many times has somebody tried to sell you something and talked about features you don't care about? By asking about three features you get enough information upon which to base a presentation. You can work other features into the presentation. I may make a comment like, "Even though this vehicle gets over 30 mpg and is very safe, boy, it's got an awful lot of power getting up to highway speeds, corners very well, and can stop on a dime." I'm not going to get real technical on performance facts for someone who's not interested.

Now for a gear-head, I'll display all I can about performance. Here's where studying product will help. You should know about increased diameter stabilizer bars, suspensions, struts, tires, and horsepower. Listen to the customer and talk to them about things they are interested in or they'll get bored and start wanting to talk about price. Pay attention to the customer or you won't solve their puzzle.

Personal Information: Do you live or work in the area?

It's important to know this information because if the customer lives nearby, he or she might consider service and convenience an important factor.

The other side of the coin is that someone might drive 30 miles and pass 10 similar dealerships to get to yours. Who knows why they did that—maybe their dad always bought cars from your dealership or they grew up in the area or once had a good experience here. The important thing is that you might get some valuable information revealing their motivations for visiting your dealership.

Sometimes they are just passing by and are trying to keep their hometown dealer honest. I'm not going to assume that, but I might consider the possibility when it comes time to ask for the sale.

I don't typically ask customers what they do for a living until they open up that door, because I don't want to pre-qualify someone based on what they do for a living. I've had some bad experiences with that. The customer might say they work at McDonalds and they're looking at a $35,000 vehicle. My attitude is shot after that. I automatically assume that they can't afford it and effectively contaminate my overall attitude about the sale. I'd rather not know. It seems like they could never afford the car, but who knows? Maybe their parents are buying it for them. I know you'll meet people who can't afford the cars you show them, and that's discouraging. Look at this way—if nothing else, its good practice, and if you give them a quality experience they might tell their friends or come back someday when they can afford it. If you're good to them, they'll ask for you when they return to the dealership.

Who is the primary driver/buyer?

When you have two people in front of you, you want to know who'll be the primary buyer. I want to know if all decision-makers are present, because I can't consummate a deal if I don't have the buyer and decision-maker in front me.

I may say, **"Will you be the primary driver?"** And then say, **"Will there be any additional drivers?"** For example, your customer may be a father buying a car for his daughter or wife; and you'll want know that detail so you can tailor your presentation with the daughter or wife in mind.

Will you be driving this car primarily for business or personal use?

I ask this question because I like to know under what conditions the buyer will be using the vehicle. I'll use myself as an example: I drive 50,000 miles per year, 90 percent for business. Based on this information, one could conclude that depreciation, gas mileage, and dependability are important to me. It is extremely important to me that the vehicles I own hold their value. As the salesperson, you can use this little bit of information to tell the buyer why the Lexus, for instance, is the right choice for him. You might say, "If you drive that many miles, the Lexus is a car that holds outstanding resale value, not to mention gets very good gas mileage and has an extremely high dependability rating."

Selling is all about saying, "This is why this car is right for you." What you need to do is find these things out and match features and benefits to the customer's desires. A good salesperson will go beyond surface information and discover benefits for the customer that the customer didn't know were there. But you have to ask the questions, or you can't discover anything.

Are you trying to stay within a particular price or payment range?

The most important reason I ask this is because I want to know if I have a price or a payment buyer. You would rather have a payment buyer, because you've got a lot more flexibility in structuring a deal. With a payment buyer you have price, trade allowance, rate, term, lease, and down payment. Ninety percent of people buy cars will finance them in some way. At some point in time, it's going to come down to payments either through leases or loans.

If the customer says he or she wants to stay around $20,000 dollars, most salespeople will demo cars just in that price range, but I'll ask one more question: "How did you arrive at that figure?" I want to get a clearer picture of their finances and the payments they can really afford. Because most of the time, that $20,000 translates into a payment scheme they got from who knows where, and if I make the mistake of not asking them how they arrived at that figure, they may go out and buy a more expensive vehicle at another dealership because they reached their payment goal. Maybe their credit union only figured for a 48-month loan and the customer really is all right with a 60-month loan.

I also ask to make sure the customer isn't way out in left field. If he wants to keep payments under $250 a month, he probably shouldn't be looking at a $40,000 Suburban unless he has a sizable down payment. The point is, get a feel for what your customers can realistically afford based on payments.

Trade-in Information: What are you driving now?

Don't ask, "What do you have to trade?" because many customers try to divide the sale into two separate transactions, one for their car and one for the new car. I guess they learned that at "car buyers school." Also, some customers might consider it a disadvantage to have a trade with more hassles and more variables to consider. I want to make the customer feel like he or she is in a good spot no matter what kind of car he or she driving now.

Did you buy that car new or used?

If the customer says he or she bought it new you can respond, "Great, my used car manager loves one-owner trade-ins." If the customer bought it used you can respond, "Has it been a good car for you? Good, because we are short in our used car inventory and we would much rather take in a car from someone like you than have go to auction or another dealership to fulfill our inventory needs."

Are both these statements true? Yes they are! I wanted to sell my own trade-ins and having information on where a car came from was helpful when selling that vehicle to another customer. Let me tell you this, there's nothing more important than a story behind a car. By knowing the history of a used vehicle, you can increase the customer's confidence in the vehicle.

You still need to stay positive even if a prospect has a real piece of junk, say an '82 Bonneville so dilapidated cats could crawl through the rust holes in the fenders. What do most salespeople say when they see something like this? They say, "You'd be better off selling that on your own." If you say that, what you're really telling them is that you don't want to do business with them. They could perceive that as an insult. Instead say, "We may not retail your vehicle because we can't warranty it. But we do deal with small dealers who specialize in vehicles in that price range. We'd love to take it in."

What I like about that car is that it won't be hard to justify trade value on it; it's not worth much, so whatever trade value you extend can be easily justified to the customer. Also, it might help get financing.

If they just have to have $2000 for the old car, they may need to be educated on the real value of their car. I might tell them they would be better off selling it themselves if they're stuck to an unrealistic trade value.

What have you enjoyed most about your car?

Whatever they love about their old car needs to be either matched or exceeded on the new one. They will say they love something about it. It could be gas mileage, ride, durability, etc., and that is the feature you'll have to replace with the car you are selling them now. You could say, "If you liked the way your old car drove (or the gas mileage, or whatever) you should really like the way this new vehicle delivers those qualities."

When I say this, I'm trying to plant seeds about important features and gather information for the next step.

Is there anything you don't like about your car?

Find out the answers to this question because that's your customers motivation for searching for a new vehicle. Maybe he or she needs more horsepower to pull a load; maybe the car has 60,000 miles and he or she doesn't like being without a warranty. Whatever the reason, it's a clue that will help you piece together the pieces to the puzzle. Work this motivation into your presentation to build value and help the customer justify making the decision to buy.

Solving the Puzzle

Qualifying is like a jigsaw puzzle. The customer walks in the door and he has a puzzle in front of him. Your job is to understand his puzzle and help him put it together one piece at a time by asking him the right questions about what he wants and need in a car. After you have assembled the puzzle you can then turn it back around and present it to them when you present the vehicle during Select and Demo and Feature/Benefit steps. What you need to do is gather information in regards to the customer's wants, needs, hot buttons and dominant buying motives and tailor your presentation towards his or her desires. If you've identified the three most important things that the customer desires, you'll be able to turn it back to the customer and say, "When we discussed features, you told me you wanted X, Y, and Z."

When you feel the product puzzle is solved, you should say something like, "Do you feel that this vehicle either meets or exceeds your expectations in all three of these areas?"

What I try to do as a salesperson is confirm, verify, and recap to remind customers of what they came in for in the beginning. I want to show them that this vehicle fulfills the needs they were looking for. When you do this it's much easier for them to say to themselves, "Yes, I guess there is no reason for me not to buy. It's everything I wanted."

Remember that the answers to everything you ask in the Qualify step will be used to help you close.

Things to remember:

- Have you spoken with any of our salespeople previously?

Product Phase of Qualifying:

- Are you interested in a new or used vehicle?
- *Are you familiar with our product line?
- Great, which model did you come to see today?
- What body style are you interested in? Do you want a 2 door, 4 door, wagon, etc . . . ?
- What basic equipment do you need on your new car?
- *Do you prefer a light, medium, or dark color?
- Great, come with me.
- What are the **three** most important things to you in the purchase of your next vehicle?

Do not ask these questions of a used car customer.

Personal Phase of Qualifying:

- Do you live or work in the area?
- Will you be using this car primarily for business or personal use?
- Who will be the primary driver?
- Will there be any additional drivers?
- Are you trying to stay within a particular price or payment range?

Trade Phase of Qualifying:

- What are you driving now? (Don't say, "What do you have to trade?")
- Did you buy that car new or used?

- What are the things that you've enjoyed most about that car?
- Is there anything that you don't like about your car?

Note:

It takes a customer approximately two weeks to get into a buying mode, but once they've started shopping, they'll usually act within 48 hours.

A Successful Sales Strategy is Flexible

Before we get into the next step, *Select and Demo,* I want to explain that there can be flexibility and overlap in the sequence in which you do particular steps. Obviously *Meet and Greet* has to be first the first step, and *Negotiate and Close* has to be last step, in between you can actually interchange things quite a bit. For example, in the Product, Personal, and Trade phases of *Qualify* that we just covered, you could actually start the *Demo* right after the Product phase and pick up the Personal and Trade phases as filler during the *Demo.* Obviously you have to complete each step, but for instance, if you're in the lot in front of the vehicles already, you might just want to jump into *Select and Demo* and finish qualifying on the demo ride. As you will see, there's also a great deal of overlap between steps 3 and 4, and the reason I break them down into separate steps is to lend clarity.

Select and Demo

Goals:

- Select the right vehicle based on the criteria gathered in Step 2, Product Phase.
- Give Interior Feature/Benefit presentation.
- Demo vehicle.
- Build value to justify price.
- Present features along with advantages and benefits.
- Tailor your presentation towards the wants and needs of the customer.

In this step we want to give an interior feature benefit presentation and ultimately demo the vehicle. The goal now is to select the correct vehicle based on your qualifying questions and then demonstrate the interior features and benefits of the car that most closely fulfills your customer's desires. Keep in mind that a vehicle properly equipped is of more importance than the color being right, so if you don't have the color your customers want, get as close as you can to the features they want.

Explain the Window Sticker

If you're selling a new car, first bring them to the car and explain how the window sticker breaks down. Make sure they understand where on the sticker the standard features are listed, and where the interior features, performance, safety, and optional features are detailed and priced. The EPA estimates and Manufacturers Suggested Retail Price (MSRP) are on the bottom. I never read the MSRP out loud, because you can be sure your customers will read it. If there is a price objection, they'll make it now. That's all right, because you haven't sold them on this particular vehicle yet; if it turns out that the price is $22,000 and the customer says that's too much, you can always bring them down to a lesser equipped vehicle.

Keep in mind the purpose of discussing the window sticker is to build value. Every time a customer receives a feature, they should understand that the value goes up. The features on the window sticker will very likely hit their hot buttons. This is the initial stage of building value to justify price.

The sticker may also show a value package showing a $500 discount because of the way the car could be ordered. You always want to point this out to the customer to plant a seed of price negotiation, anticipation. If the customer wants a $2,000 discount you can say, "Remember, in the beginning I told you that the vehicle was discounted $500, which ultimately decreases our margins. There isn't as much discount to work with because they've given you a $500 discount up front." What the customer should realize is that they've already received a $500 discount, and in effect they should expect a lesser discount in the end. If you plant that seed right away, it's going to stick with your customer, and you can use it in negotiate and close.

Demo

The process works like this: Go to the window sticker to verify and confirm (verify it's the right vehicle and confirm that it's properly equipped). After verifying and confirming the sticker categories, you should say, "I'll be right back; I'm going to grab the keys so that you can see the inside of the car." Not so they customer can drive it. Get the keys and come back and bring the customer to the passenger front door. Open the passenger door and say, "Have a seat; I want to share with you some of the interior features on this vehicle."

Why do I bring the customer to the passenger seat? Because the salesperson wants to drive the car first. Why? Because there are two seats in the front of the car: one of them is threatening and one of them is not. The threatening seat is behind the wheel. If I put the customer behind the wheel, I have to ask, "Do you want to drive the car?" I risk hearing **no** at that point, so I'm going to be very assumptive about it and put the customer in the passenger seat. Get in the driver's seat, start the vehicle, and begin your interior feature benefit presentation.

Interior Feature Benefit Presentation
Things to cover while in the car

To better illustrate what I mean, let's discuss in depth a few more safety features to discover how to demonstrate features and benefits. These are good examples of newer features that have become popular on many cars and should be explained so that the customer understands they are getting a better car now than they got in the past. Customers may not be aware of new features that have come on the scene, and it's your job to tell them. Customize your interior presentation for them. If they expressed an interest in safety, for instance, start off by sharing safety features.

Airbags

I always start out with airbags and give a short explanation on how airbag systems work. I explain that there are sensors in the front bumper, and in the event of a frontal collision, or near frontal collision, of approximately 18mph or greater, the airbags will deploy. They inflate in 1/20th of a second and stay inflated for only one second with the air released from perforations in the bag. You can also talk about side airbags if applicable.

When people become aware, familiar, and educated on how something works, it increases the value of the feature and their overall comfort level. The more they know about something the more comfortable they are. Does that make sense? And this goes for any other feature you could name. If they don't know what something does, it holds no value for them and they're not willing to pay for it. Your product knowledge is very important at this stage of the game and will really help build value. In the end, your customers will understand all of the dollars of research and development that it took to design and develop features for them and their family.

Anti-Lock Brake Systems (ABS)

Another feature to explain might be ABS. I always ask the customer if they currently drive a vehicle with ABS or if they have ever driven one. I want to know that, because many customers who first experience what happens when anti-lock brakes engage are scared out of their wits. They dodn't know what to expect. For example, once while in the service department of a client dealership, I witnessed an older lady come in to complain about her brakes. She was just frantic; I thought she was going to have a heart attack. The roads were icy and slippery that day, and she said, "Oh, my brakes are going out, there's this terrible pounding underneath my foot and it's making a loud thumping noise." Unfamiliar with ABS, she didn't know what she had described was normal operation. When she bought the car, the salesperson didn't bother to demonstrate or explain what would happen when the ABS was engaged. She was really shaken up.

In contrast, during a demo ride for those unfamiliar with ABS, I find a safe but slippery parking lot and say, "Folks, your seat belts are on, I want you to brace yourself. I'm going to engage the anti-lock brakes so you can experience what's going to happen." I went on to explain that ABS worked using an onboard computer in the braking system. It automatically sensed brake lock up and pumped the brakes 8-10 times per second dual diagonally. In addition, I would paint a picture saying, "I don't know if you're ever had it happen folks, that you were driving down the road and you had to slam on your brakes and the back end whipped around on you. Well, that doesn't happen with anti-lock brakes. What happens in those situations is that you are hydroplaning on ice, snow, or water. ABS will keep you and your family safe."

Driver and Passenger Protection

Tell customers about steel I-beams inside the doors. These I-beams can sustain up to 33-mph side impact before they will collapse into the driver or passenger compartment. These are federal standards that perhaps your customers don't know about. Other models may have different numbers. Demonstrate by placing your hand or fist where the steel beams are located on doors and roofs.

Another effective safety word track could go like this: "When Chrysler designed this vehicle, they designed it with a double steel roof. It's part of the safety cage construction. This roof can support 1.5 times the weight of the vehicle in the event of a rollover. God forbid it would happen, but it would at least keep your family safe."

Other Features

Also talk about any other features that you feel are important. Some of you have options/features that are exclusive to your particular make and model. If your customers have kids, you might want to talk about the master on/off switch for power windows, or the childproof door locks in the back. Try to hit hot buttons you think might be important to them based on their driving habits or lifestyles.

Test Drive – Demo Route

After presenting the interior features of the car, I ask if the customers have any questions regarding these features. If not, I ask them to buckle their seat belts, sit back, relax, and enjoy the ride while I drive. Be very assumptive. Put on your own seat belt and start moving. They are going to do one of two things: they will either say they don't want a test drive, or they will strap on their seatbelts. Don't forget to get your dealer plates, copy of their driver's license, or whatever your dealership requires.

You should always have a pre-planned demo route. Know where you're going before you leave. If possible, tailor the demo ride towards the strengths of the vehicle. If I'm taking someone out in a Honda Prelude, Chevy Camero, or Ford Mustang, I want curvy roads that accentuate the performance strengths of the vehicle. If I'm in a Bonneville or Cadillac, I'll find bumpy roads to demo the smooth and quiet ride.

Then you need to get to a parking lot. If possible, find a place with some scenic beauty such as a lake or park. Find a nice backdrop because you're trying to paint a picture and create interest in ownership. A spot with natural beauty is a great place to switch seats, or if appropriate, give an Exterior Feature/Benefit presentation before switching. I also think that you're much more effective at selling when you're not within the confines of the dealership. Are people more comfortable inside or outside the dealership? Usually. They'll retain more information and have a longer attention span when they are outside the dealership. After getting to the parking lot I say, "Now it's your turn." Get out and ask them to take the driver's seat.

NOTE: *If appropriate and the weather permits, start Step 4 Exterior Feature/Benefit Presentation before you switch seats. Be flexible and at ease.*

Make the Customer Comfortable

I won't leave the driver side of the car until the customer is tucked into the driver's seat and it fits them like a glove. If for any reason he or she is uncomfortable, if there are blind spots, or if the mirror is not adjusted correctly, he or she won't have the comfort level needed to make the decision to buy the car. If you have an eight-way power seat, get the customer exactly the way he or she wants. Demonstrate how. Set the tilt steering and make sure he or she is close enough to the brake pedal.

Another little thing that can make a big difference is the radio station. Ask your customers which station they normally listen to and tune the radio to that station. Show them where the volume is and tell them to feel free to adjust it. Once again, I'm trying to create an atmosphere of ownership here by getting customers as comfortable as possible and also demonstrating the great stereo system. Get everything tuned in before you take off.

If I have a buyer and a co-buyer, I'll try to get the co-buyer into the front seat and I'll sit in back. Open the door and say something like, "Mary why don't you go ahead and sit in front?" If she objects, your response could be, "When you and Bill are riding together, aren't you normally riding in the front seat? Doesn't it make more sense to experience the vehicle from where you'll typically sit?" Now she's in the front seat and I'm in the back, exactly what I want. Hopefully, they'll switch positions during the demo ride. If they ask where to go, encourage them to drive under the conditions they normally drive. For instance, drive the highway and test accelerating onto highway ramps, or drive corners or bumpy roads. Suggest a route that displays the strengths of the car.

Zip your Lip

This is the only time during the sales process that I believe you should be silent, other than after asking a closing question. I want customers focusing completely on the car, because this is where the heat starts building as they're driving and smelling the new car smell and playing with all the toys. I don't want them distracted by a salesperson asking questions. If they initiate conversation, I'll respond simply. I won't start anything but rather let them talk between themselves and experience the car in solitude without distraction. That's a very effective strategy.

Park Next to Their Trade

Upon returning to the dealership I don't believe in putting the car back where it came from. Here's why: First, they've never parallel parked this car, so they'll probably park it crooked and I'll have to straighten it out later. Second, I want to give an exterior feature benefit presentation, if I didn't do it before, and I want them to experience the exterior from more than two-feet away. I don't want them rubbing against other cars, getting their clothes dirty, or worse, dinging doors. They should have a better perspective than that. Additionally, if you can get them to park it next to their trade, that's effective because it'll reinforce the positive benefits the new car has over the old one. If you are going to present exterior features, ask them now to pop the hood and the trunk before leaving the driver's seat.

FAB Selling—Feature/Advantage/Benefit

Throughout the *Demo* process, a customer needs to understand what advantages and benefits the features of the car will give them in order to understand the value of the car. For example, if I were to say to you, "Here's a dry erase marker: assuming you had a need for it, what would you pay for it?" Thirty-five cents. What if I went on to say that one of the advantages of this marker was that it had an ounce of gold in the barrel and was the only one of its kind in the world? The value of the marker just went way up when I explained a hidden advantage/benefit.

Every time you demo a feature you should explain the advantages and benefits, because what good is a feature if it doesn't have a use? Describing features along with advantages and benefits is where you raise the value. Our job as professional salespeople is to raise the value to where it either meets or exceeds price. A feature's value is not always readily apparent to customers and must be explained. The best salespeople, the highest average gross salespeople, are those who give thorough presentations and build value to justify price. When customers can appreciate that your car has advantages over the competition, they will come closer to buying.

Become a product specialist. You really need to make that commitment because it will give you confidence and the customer will accordingly have confidence in you. If you don't know something about the car, admit you don't know it, don't fake your way through. Say, "Folks, I don't know the answer to that, but I have someone inside that can certainly get the answer." They'll respect you more than if you try to buffalo them. Just be honest. Study the product and become confident.

Conclusions

Why do such a good job on demonstrating the features and benefits of the car? Many times in a closing situation I'll ask a customer, "Let me ask you this, because obviously this is how I make my living: you've shopped at four different stores; how would you rate your experience here in comparison to the other stores?" They always say it was the best!

Why ask? Because I know I rolled out the red carpet for them. I treated them like royalty. When a customer walks into a dealership, he or she should come to expect this kind of treatment and accept nothing less. They deserve it. I train customers on how to buy and what they should expect. Buying a car is a major decision in their life, and I know it's not an easy one. If I do my job, it can stop them from shopping any further, especially if they've already been to three or four other stores. Eventually, I ask everybody to buy, but I'm not going to ask until I've earned the right and the time is right.

Things to remember:
- Explain window sticker.
- Keys, demo plate, copy of driver's license.
- Customer in passenger seat—you drive.
- Pre-planned demo route.
- Present features/benefits throughout step.
- Switch seats in safe, scenic place.
- Make customer comfortable in the driver's seat.
- Zip lips while the customer drives.
- Park next to trade.

Feature/Benefit

Goals:

- Give Exterior Feature/Benefit presentation at each of the first five positions.
- Tailor your presentation towards the wants and needs of the customer.
- Continue to build value to justify price.
- Begin to Overcome Objections.

Six-Step Walk Around

Goals in this step are to give an exterior feature and benefit presentation. In the industry it's commonly called the Six-Step Walk Around. At each of six positions you'll talk about certain features of the car. See the illustration on the next page.

Tailor your Exterior Feature/Benefit presentation towards your customer's wants, needs, dominant buying motives and hot buttons that you have identified during the previous step. Let's touch on some features for each position.

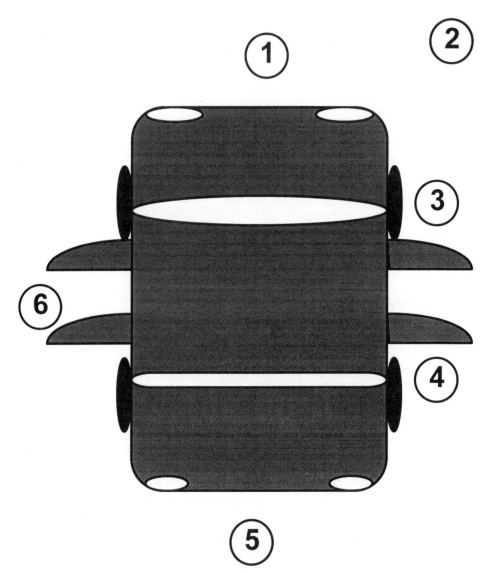

Position 1: Under the Hood

To start you can talk about the **double hood latch** feature. It's minor but important. I had the hood fly up on me once while driving on the freeway. It makes a good story and some customers don't really know how it works.

Maintenance free batteries are on most cars these days. Explain to them that green indicates a full charge and a dark shade warns them the battery is going bad.

Describe the **crumple zones** in the front for safety. Hoods and fenders are now designed with notches or indentations in the metal, so in the event of a frontal collision the front of the car collapses in accordion-style, so you aren't shoving sheet metal back through the windshield or blocking your view. It's also more energy absorbing and a safer design.

A **dual diagonal braking system** is also great feature to explore. The brain box to the braking system is in the master cylinder. Modern brakes have two separate reservoirs of brake fluid. The two brake lines are independent, and the front right wheel is tied to the left rear wheel and likewise on the other side; hence the term dual-diagonal. In the event of a broken brake line, you'll still have braking power on at least one front and one rear wheel at all times because of this safety feature.

In addition, modern brakes now have a flutter valve so that in the event you lose power or run out of gas, you still have brakes. If you lost power before you would lose your power steering and the brake pedal felt like a rock. That doesn't happen anymore because the flutter valve keeps enough vacuum pressure in the system so you can pump the brakes 8-10 times and come to a safe stop.

The **onboard computer** automatically monitors all the engine operations in the event that something isn't running to its optimum efficiency. When the check engine light comes on, a service technician can easily hook the engine to his diagnostic equipment and read the code from the diagnostic computer, which will tell him exactly what's wrong with the car. This system ultimately reduces the cost of ownership because once the car is out of warranty, you have to pay for diagnostic time, which can be $70-$100 per hour. Without the onboard computer, it could take them three hours to find a problem, you might have to pay more than $200 versus a half an hour with the onboard computer and a modern diagnostic system. In the end, this feature helps a technician diagnose a problem properly and quickly.

Vehicle **warranties** are an important feature, and this is a good time to explain the warranties that come with the car. Know the details of the warranty for new or used cars. It might be a 3-year, 36,000-mile bumper-to-bumper zero-deductible warranty, or a 5-year 50,000-mile emissions warranty. If you sell GM or Ford, for instance, all models have the same new car warranties, so you only have to learn it once for each manufacturer.

If you're selling a used car, go the to buyers guide instead of the new car sticker. Try to increase your customers comfort level by telling him or her the details of the used car warranty. If your dealership has enough confidence to put a warranty on it, your customer will have more confidence in buying it.

Some cars offer **roadside assistance**. If you're selling Chevys, for instance, there's a toll-free 1-800-chevusa number that owners can use 24 hours a day, 365 days a year, if they run out of gas, stall, or lock their keys in the car. It's included in the warranty. That's a pretty great feature, and you should mention it.

Position 2: Front Passenger Side

The first thing you notice when looking at a car from this particular angle is the **aerodynamic styling**. The advantage is there is less coefficient of drag. In other words, the vehicle moves through the air more cleanly, which increases the gas mileage and reduces wind noise. Along with that, many are designed with **low hood lines** that slope down in the front. As the car accelerates, more down-force will be created, and this in turn produces a more stable driving environment.

Halogen headlamps are now pretty standard. Of course they're brighter, last longer, and are cheaper to replace than traditional lights. Originally, a sealed beam halogen light could cost as much as $90. Now they only cost $8 to $10 because you are only buying the bulb.

Now is a good time to mention the **five-mile-per-hour front bumper**. They are made of a composite material, not metal, and they rebound to their original shape on collisions of 5 miles per hour or less. It's a small feature, but nice to have.

Position 3: Right Front Wheel/Right Front Door

I sold Hondas in the early 80s and within the first three years the front fenders began rusting out. Now, with plastic **inner fender liners**, cars don't deteriorate as fast. In cold climates, where sand, salt, and chemicals are used on the roads, the shock towers and chassis used to rust out and cause serious damage. Now, composite panels make the car look better and increase the resale value because they won't rust, dent, or ding. Remember, don't just tell your customers what the feature is, but tell them what it does to increase the overall value of the car.

Position 4: Rear Door

Show them the **childproof door locks** and how to work the lever on the inside of the door that engages the device. For parents with young children, this is an essential feature.

This is also a good place to talk about **visibility**. Visibility is a safety feature that many manufacturers have really begun to stress. For example, when the new Chrysler minivan was introduced, it boasted 30% more visibility. What designers are trying to do is make the pillars supporting the windows thinner and thinner in each model. This reduces blind spots and makes it easier to switch lanes and parallel park. This can be a hot button for shorter people or the elderly who might not see as well as they used to.

Rear window defrosters are also a nice safety and convenience feature. Many are now on timers, and when the rear window reaches a certain temperature will automatically shut off.

Know your tires. **M&S** stands for mud and snow tires, and if the car is equipped with four-season radials, tell your customers they won't have to buy snow tires.

Position 5: Rear

The **high mounted stop lamp** is a mandatory safety feature on every car, van, and light duty truck since 1994. Studies have shown that rear end collisions are greatly reduced as the result of having a third tail lamp at eye level.

I've never been one to quote 14.7 cubic feet of **cargo capacity** or anything like that, because I don't think anyone can identify with what that means. But what I do say is, "I remember the first time I looked at this car and I envisioned how big the trunk was going to be; I was amazed when I opened it up. As you can see, folks, they've utilized all the available space in the trunk by putting the space saver spare underneath and mounting the jack to the sidewall." Mention when trunks have low entries, you don't have to lift cargo so high. It's so much more convenient to get objects in and out. Some cars have **split fold or fold down rear seats**. This increases the versatility of what you can carry. Pontiac has a center pass through the rear armrests in some models in case you've got to carry two-by-fours, hockey sticks, skis, or anything else extra long.

You've also got **crumple zones** in the back that collapse in an accordion style to protect rear passengers, as well as a **5-mile per hour bumper**.

Mention rear window wiper/washers on vans and utility vehicles. If your customers have never had them before, they'll be amazed at how great they are at increasing visibility and safety in difficult weather, especially on muddy or wet roads.

Position 6: At Driver's Door

Make sure you know whether or not the customer has a trade at this point. Because if he or she is are trading, now is the logical time to proceed to *Step 5: Trade Evaluation.* If your customers aren't trading, you should continue to confirm and verify and deal with objections. If, on the other hand, they are trading, go get a trade evaluation, then come back to continue the "confirm and verify" portion of this step.

Confirm and Verify

At the driver's door, confirm and verify and go through a recap process. I say to the customer, "Well, what did you think of the car? Did you like it? Did you like the way it rode and drove?" You might talk about things that you know are positive and that you know the customer enjoyed based on comments they made.

Here is your opportunity to turn the puzzle around for them. For instance say, "Remember back in the beginning, you said to me that the three most important things to you in the purchase of you next vehicle were X, Y, and Z. Do you feel this vehicle either meets or exceeds your expectations in all those areas?"

Let me repeat that question: **"Do you feel this vehicle either meets or exceeds your expectations in all those areas?"**

The reason I repeat the question is because people come in with all kinds of barriers in front of them that prevent them from saying yes, and I want to go back and confirm that this is what they came in looking for and that I have delivered all of the things that are most important to them. It's easier to make a decision when we go back and confirm and verify that the vehicle is properly equipped and meets or exceeds their expectations, that it satisfies all their wants and needs. That's why it's so vitally important that you go back and confirm and verify before you ask the first closing question.

Getting a Mental Commitment

"Well, seeing as how you like the car so much, let me ask you this: 'Can you picture yourself in this vehicle?'" And the customer says, "Yes that's an awfully nice car." "Okay, so what you're telling me is you feel we've selected the right vehicle for you today." And they'd say, "Yes, I think it's equipped the way we want it." I say, "Great, because that's the hardest part of my job." In other words, after finding just the right vehicle, the rest is easy. If the customer is affirmative here, I'm going to go after a trial close and get a mental commitment for the vehicle. I'll only do this if I have the buyer and all decision-makers present.

A good word track for a trial close: **"Seeing as how you like the car so much, let me ask you this—If we work out all the details to your satisfaction, can I tell my boss we could earn your business now?"**

There are two different kinds of commitments involved in a car deal. One is a mental commitment, and one is a financial commitment. This is a mental commitment. It's saying, I like you, I like the car, I like the dealership. . . if I like the numbers, I'll do business with you now.

The mental commitment has nothing to do with price and numbers right now; however, the mental commitment has to come before the financial one ever does. A financial commitment would be when the customer says, I'll pay 20 grand for that car. These are two separate commitments; first get them sold on the vehicle they want, then on the price.

Three Possible Responses

Now, there are only three possible responses to the question, "If we work out all the details to your satisfaction, can I tell the boss I can earn your business now?" The answers are yes, maybe, or no, and here's the best way to deal with each.

Yes

If the customer says yes, shut up and proceed to the next steps. You asked a closing question and got the response you wanted—stop selling! A lot of people talk too much. They talk their way into a deal and right back out of it again. When you ask a closing question zip, your lip when you get the right response. Talk about anything other than the car, because you've gotten a mental commitment. At this point you've found the right car and can proceed to the dealership walk and appraisal steps.

Maybe

Maybe can be turned into a yes if you ask the right question. I ask what they mean by maybe. They might respond, "I don't even know what your boss would sell me the car for." In that case, you have to clarify that the numbers are a separate issue, and that they are committing only to that particular car at this point. Repeat to them, "If you like the numbers, are you prepared to make a decision right now?" You want a firm yes, nothing wishy-washy. So they will clearly understand you want them to repeat, "If I like the numbers, I will do business with you now." Turn the maybe into a yes.

No

Sometimes they say no, which is a problem most salespeople really mishandle because they don't know where to go. Now all of a sudden we're dealing with an objection. No is an objection, isn't it? Initial objections often come at this point, and you have to verify whether or not it's a feature of the car or another factor that causes the objection.

Isolate and Overcome Objections

We'll talk much more about objections in step seven, *Negotiate and Close,* but let's briefly touch on the initial objection stage. There are two kinds of objections: stated objections and real objections. Stated objections are no more than smoke screens, stalls, and excuses. They are valid only about 20 percent of the time, and the other 80 percent are an avoidance tool. I look at receiving stated objections from a customer like playing Frisbee with them, with me catching objection after objection with no end in sight. Inexperienced salespeople risk trying to overcome objection after objection after objection, but what they really need to do is put the customer in a corner and find out the real objection, which is the final objection. You always close on the final objection.

You need to cut to the chase and discover the final objection as soon as you can. My point is this: Within the first two months of selling cars, you'll have heard every objection you're ever going to hear. Now that should give you confidence. Why? Because we already know what the customer is going to say before he or she walks in the door. How much easier can it get? Think about it for a second—we already know they are going to say your price is too high; they need to think about it; they need to talk to a spouse; they need to talk to a banker; they need more for their trade; the payments are too high. If we already know what they are going to say, as professional salespeople it's our responsibility to have as many ways to overcome these objections as possible.

I believe it's impossible for a part-time buyer to out-maneuver a full-time salesperson. That's my attitude about it—a little cocky, I know, but the bottom line is I know what the customer is going to say before he or she walks in the door.

You always close on the final objection, and a way to discover that is to ask directly. For instance a good word track after an initial no is **"Well, I'm sure you have a reason for feeling that way. Do you mind if I ask what it is?"**

Now, they'll have an objection here, and a good word track for you to practice is, **"Other than the fact that (repeat the objection), is that the only thing holding you back from making a decision right now?"** It might go something like this, "Other than the fact that (you need to talk with your wife, or it's the first place you've shopped, or it's the wrong color, or whatever the objection might be), is that the only thing holding you back from making a decision right now? I want to isolate the objections here and boil them down to one single objection if I can.

This is part of turning the puzzle back to the customer, because you can always say, "But you told me that if (X, Y, or Z objection were satisfied) you would be prepared to make a deal." You need to take them through this process to get them to a final objection, now that we know we only have one objection to deal with.

Make the commitment to prepare yourself. Do a post-mortem after every *up*. Analyze the objections you receive and ask successful salespeople how they deal with particular objections. If they sell 20-25 cars a month, obviously they aren't getting stuck on some of the objections that cause you problems. It make sense that once a customer or prospect leaves your dealership without buying, you reached an impasse of some kind that you couldn't overcome. Doesn't it also make sense to go to your managers or top salespeople and ask for help? They've heard all the objections and have answers for them all. Get ammunition from different salespeople. They obviously know how to overcome these objections or they wouldn't be selling 20-25 cars a month.

Think about this: Each and every time you meet a prospect, a sale is made. Either they sell you that they're not buying or you sell them that they are.

Things to remember:

- Six step walk around.
- Confirm and verify.
- "Do you feel that this vehicle either meets or exceeds your expectations?"
- Getting a mental commitment, not a financial commitment.
- "If we work out all the details to your satisfaction can I tell my. .boss we could earn your business now?"
- Turn maybe into a yes.
- Isolate and overcome initial objections.

Trade Evaluation

Goals:

- Evaluate the trade based on its condition, not its value.
- Educate the customer about the criteria used to determine the value of a used vehicle.

The goals in this step are to learn how to justify a trade value based on its condition only, not on its value, and also educate the customer about the criteria used to determine the value of a used vehicle. For most of you, Appraisal is really Trade Evaluation, because the managers are going to be the ones who assign a price valuation to the trade vehicle. I think that one of the biggest stumbling blocks you could have as a salesperson is inability to justify trade allowance. We lose a lot of car deals because salespeople just flatly state, "My boss is willing to pay $5,000 for your vehicle." Period— end of discussion, with absolutely no justification as to why.

The customer has to understand the logic behind a trade evaluation and where you are coming from when you present a number. It's also important to have the customer with you when doing the evaluation in order to get the customer to think realistically about their trade. So many of us just get stuck and don't know what to say when the customer says "That's not enough for my trade." If you have no ammunition with which to counter that objection, you need to get some.

A good place to start is to let the customer know that there is an expense entailed when reconditioning a trade for resale that will affect the appraised value of the trade. In other words, if a car was worth $5,000, but now needs reconditioning costing $500, then you're going to bid that car for $4,500. I always want to let the customer know that we know what's wrong with the car in regards to dings, dents, scratches, rock chips, rust spots, etc.

I understand some cars don't need a lot of reconditioning, but regardless of the inside or outside condition, we are still going to do a time-consuming inspection on the car before we issue a used car warranty. On virtually every used car, the dealership spends $400 to $600 on a thorough reconditioning and inspection. That's part of the justification for trade allowances and should be pointed out to the customer during "negotiate and close."

Most customers want retail for their used trade, and that's just not possible. They may need an explanation that the dealership can't stay in business if they own their vehicles for retail.

You need an appraisal form, and you need the customer to come with you during the appraisal. Understand that the information you gather on this form generates a legal document. So when you're writing vehicle identification numbers (VIN), serial numbers, mileage, plate numbers and expiration, etc., take your time and make sure you get it right. Because if you get it wrong, you'll end up having to redo the paperwork, which is a hassle for the customer. This is a bad experience and could affect your customer satisfaction index. So never hurry through the appraisal form.

Always go to the serial number first, because you want to verify the year of the car and can do that by reading the 10th digit of the serial number. The 10th digit tells you the model year. Verify it now by using the following chart:

Year of vehicle (10th digit)

A= 80	B=81	C=82	D=83	E=84	F=85
G=86	H=87	J=88	K=89	L=90	M=91
N=92	P=93	R=94	S=95	T=96	V=97
W=98	X=99	Y=00	1=01	2=02	3=03

I like the appraisal forms that have 17 boxes on them because there are 17 digits on every automobile's serial number since 1980. It's important to know the year of the car from the serial number because sometimes the customer tells you the wrong year and you'll want to verify with them the correct year. Ask them if they have the title or registration so you can confirm the vehicle is a 1996, for example. Sometimes they just don't know the correct year if the model has stayed the same.

Do a **"silent walk-around"** the car. In other words, you don't have to say a word. The way you need to approach this particular part of the step is to look at the vehicle like you're buying it yourself. What would you look for? How's the tire tread depth? Are there dings, dents, rust, scratches, chips, cracked headlights or taillights, or cracked windshields? Once you're finished looking, rub scratches to see if they are surface or deep. These are things the dealership will want to fix, and it's going to cost money to do that, plus you want the customer to know that you know what's wrong with their car.

After walking all the way around the car and noting imperfections, get the keys and start it so you can check the engine and transmission. Ask the customer to sit in the passenger seat of the car, and you get in the driver's seat. You should test the power windows and door locks and make sure the air-conditioning blows cold. Make sure the exhaust isn't loud and noisy. Shift into drive, park, and reverse and make sure there's no clunking or slipping into gear. Does the engine run smoothly or is it missing? Does the power seat work? Just play with everything and make sure it works. Are there any tears or rips in the upholstery, or cracks in the dash? Are there any broken knobs, or do the radio speakers crackle because one of them is blown? Does everything work inside the car? These are things the next buyer will want to have fixed, so the dealership will have to fix them before putting the car on the lot.

After checking the operation of all features, ask the following questions:

- When did you buy the car?
- Where did you buy it?
- How often did you service it? Oil every 3000 miles? Where did you get that done?
- Was the vehicle ever rust proofed and undercoated?
- Is there any warranty remaining on it?
- Have you ever done any major mechanical repairs? Do you have receipts? If the transmission is rebuilt, that's certainly of value to the next customer. Has the engine been replaced?
- Would you recommend it?
- Can I give your number to a prospective buyer?
- Is there anything more that you can tell me about your car that will help me sell it to my boss?
- Is there any balance owed? Approximately how much? To whom do you make your payments?

The reason I ask all these questions is because there are two ways to bring this car to my used car manager. The first is to say, "Hey boss, I got a '98 Ford Taurus with 48,000 miles on it." Then, just hand over the appraisal card. That's the way most salespeople do it.

A better method is to tell your boss you have a '98 Ford Taurus with 48,000 miles; the people bought it new at this dealership, so it's a one-owner; they've done all the factory recommended services and they've done it in our service department, so we've got a file with all the service information. They rust proofed and undercoated it when it was new, and they bought a 5-year, 60,000-mile extended warranty, so there's still 12,000 miles left on the warranty. They've never done any major mechanical repairs because it's been a very good car; and they wouldn't have a problem with someone giving them a call regarding its condition.

Which car is worth more to you? The second, right? Though it's the same car, it sounds a lot more appealing when you get the real history behind the car. To me, nothing is better than a used car with a story behind it. I want to sell this car, and as a used car manager I want to have it on my lot. I'll step up to the plate for the right car, with the right history and I especially wanted to sell the cars that were one-owner trades that I had sold new.

I'll warn you though; some used car managers will get irritated when you do that. They think you are trying to sell to the wrong person and unnecessarily build up the customer's expectations. Check on how they feel about it. Personally, I never felt that way. If there is a story behind a car that will enhance its value, I want it told, and I especially want to reward repeat customers who use the dealership for service and take care of their vehicles. A thorough investigation on the history of the car would certainly give me more confidence that I would want that car in my lot.

When you ask about warranties on your appraisal, you are also planting a seed that will help your dealership sell a warranty on the new car. If an extended warranty gives value to a trade, it will give value to a new car, too. I want all of my customers to buy an extended warranty because I don't want to deal with the uncertainty, and I also want insurance against irate and disappointed customers.

For instance, when I buy a used vehicle, I get a certified one. Many have an extended warranty all the way up to 100,000 miles. I'm covered for up to 100,000 miles on that car because it's certified. Most manufacturers now have "Certified" programs.

Gaining an edge with used car knowledge.

I tried to get educated on every used car on the lot by checking the trade-in book each morning to see what deals were written so I knew what trades were coming in. I also walked the used car lot every other day.

I used to tell people when they were looking for used cars to give me a call with a 30-day window of when they wanted a car; then I could cherry-pick a car for them. If I took a car in and wouldn't be delivering the new one until the next day, I would call the person waiting in the wings and tell him everything I could about the car, color, mileage, condition, etc. I'd also say, if you want an opportunity at it, this vehicle isn't going to last long in the lot. I'm going to come over to your house tonight and get a $100 hold check, and we're going to write up a deal pending you seeing the vehicle. This is a great thing to do if your dealership allows it.

I'd have the deal written and the deposit on it before the car even hit the lot. That's a car I want to sell as a salesperson, and that's just one of the things I did to get ahead of the competition. Let's face it, what happens with the nicest cars? Poof—they are gone in 24 hours. They just are. That's the kind of car you'd love to sell when you know the whole history, and that's a good reason to do a thorough trade evaluation. Make sure the customer knows that you know the condition of the trade, because it will help you justify the trade allowance. Find out all that you can about the trade, because it will help if you ever get the opportunity to sell it to another customer. Be thorough in your evaluation, because you don't want to go back and do it again.

Things to remember:

- Have the customer present when you look at trade.
- Fill out Appraisal Form thoroughly.
- Verify model year from serial number on the car.
- Conduct a Silent Walk-Around.
- Get keys and start car with customer in the passenger seat.
- Check AC, radio, exhaust, power windows, locks, seats, engine, transmission, interior condition, etc.
- Ask list of questions: "There's nothing more important than a story behind a used car."
- Plant seeds to sell an extended warranty on the car you're selling.

Dealership Walk

Goal:

- Sell service.
- Build confidence in the dealership.

In step six, your goal is to sell service, because service is important to customers. The Dealership Walk can happen while the used car manager or appraiser is with the customer's trade or at another time, whatever is appropriate for your dealership. During the walk, you should to educate the customer on the advantages of doing business with your dealership after the sale and build their confidence in the overall competence of your dealership.

In order to sell the service department, the best suggestion I can give you is to get to know the men and women in the garage. Go to the service manager and ask him, "If you were selling your service department to a customer, what would you tell them about it?"

They are going to list things like extended hours, car washes, rental cars, fully enclosed drive through, loaner cars, shuttle bus, body shop, million dollar parts inventory, five star award winning service center, 10 factory certified technicians with more than 100 years of combined experience, etc. In short, all the things that will make your service department more convenient and reliable for the customer over the little fixit shop on the corner.

A word track I used was, "Folks, is service important to you? Well, let me share with you some of the advantages of doing business with ABC Motors after the sale." Keep in mind these people will spend more time in the service department during the ownership period than they do in the sales department, and you want to enlist them as comfortable, repeat customers.

The other thing I'd like you to do is develop a strong relationship with the service writers and technicians. Sometimes this department can look at the "suits" in the sales department with a little resentment, and in turn employees can let walls build up between departments in the dealership. Let them know you appreciate them, because the bottom-line is that if your customers aren't happy with the service, you won't get the chance to sell them their next car.

I did little things for service technicians. For instance, if I had a customer that came in repeatedly because a tricky problem couldn't be fixed and the technician finally solved the problem, or my customer made a positive comment about how well they had been treated by a technician, heck, I'd bring them a 12 pack of beer or soda as thanks for the extra effort. Once I bought three technicians dealership jackets. Yes, I spent $50 bucks on each of them, and it was well worth it, because these people really helped me throughout the year. If I were on a demo ride with a used car and there was a problem, I'd pull into the garage and these technicians would break away from whatever they were doing and help me and tell me what was wrong or what they thought was wrong. Or, if I had a trade that was getting appraised and it had an apparent problem, I'd bring it back to service to get an idea of what it would cost to fix. I developed a good, strong relationship with the people in service, and in return for my appreciation, they passed their referrals onto me. I sold cars to their friends and families too.

I received most of the referrals out of the back end of the store because of the relationships that I had established with these people. They are very important people to me, and they should be to you. The fact of the matter is, it all goes back to attitude management. If you treat people in other departments the way you'd like to be treated, good things are going to happen for you. Your customers will sense the good relationships during the dealership walk, and that will spill over into a smoother car deal. Introduce a customer to service personnel if it seems appropriate. The more rapport you build with the whole operation, the better for you.

Though it's a short step, it's very important. If you have a clean shop with an enclosed drive-through, it's impressive and you should show it off. When customers see a spotless shop with neat technicians in a well lighted and organized environment, they get the impression that quality work is being done here.

Smooth relationships between sales and service are important, and it's no different with the Finance and Insurance (F&I) department, which we'll talk about in Step 8 when we cover Turn Over (T.O.).

Things to Remember:

- Parts
- Body Shop
- Extended Hours
- Loaner/Rental Vehicles
- Shuttle Van
- Fully Enclosed Check-in Lane
- Technical Credentials and Awards Earned
- Smooth Relationships

Negotiate and Close Overcoming Objections

Goals:

- Transfer a mental commitment to paper.
- Overcome the five most common price objections.
- Learn the Step Down Method.
- Solicit the best offer you can.
- Learn additional closing techniques.

The number one goal in this step is to close the deal and make the sale. In order to do that, you'll need to overcome customer objections and come to an agreement on price. Your first task is to get the customer's verbal commitment, that is, mental commitment, on paper. Earlier in the sales process, you asked the question, "If we can work out the details to your satisfaction, may I tell my boss that we can earn your business today?" The customer has responded "yes" and you've confirmed and verified and done the dealership walk and gotten a mental commitment. Now it's time to get to your office because, "You sell on your feet and you close on your seat."

When you have a mental commitment at the end of step four or five, depending on whether or not you have a trade, get back to your office and fill out the buyer's worksheet completely, with the buyer present. You'll need to bring it to your manager to begin *Step 7: Negotiate and Close.*

On your worksheet, write the following statement in the first open spot on the worksheet "Mr. & Mrs. Smith will own and take delivery of (name vehicle) when the figures are agreeable." Get the mental commitment on paper and formally confirm it. Then turn the form around to them and ask the customer to "give me your OK here." Now you have formalized their mental commitment and you're ready to get numbers from your boss.

Making the Initial Offer

Some of you may have managers that also want you to solicit a beginning offer from the buyer rather than just a commitment to buy now. You'll know quickly if your store wants this. I prefer the dealership make the initial offer because it takes the pressure off the customer to come up with an initial offer and leaves the buyer in a less threatening position. Remember, their biggest fear is paying too much, and if we ask them to make the first offer, how often are we going to be in the black on their initial offer? Almost never. Ninety-nine percent of the time they start with such a low offer that we'll have a huge hill to climb just to get to a minimally acceptable gross on the deal.

If you start with their number, then they will have set the level for negotiation, but on the other hand, if I ask my boss to start the deal, then we have set the level for negotiation. When they make the first offer, every time they come up, they lose, but when we set the first number, every time we come down, they win. We also want to start at a price that allows us to make an acceptable profit.

It's also a good position for you as the salesperson not to accept personal responsibility for the numbers. They are always your boss's numbers. I don't want the customers to blame me for the numbers, so I don't want to start the numbers. Unless they are paying the window sticker price, I can't approve the deal, anyway. I used to say to people that price is a function of management. I said, "I'm sure there are decisions on your job that you can't make, and this is one on my job that I can't make." Put them in a place they can identify with. I don't want the responsibility of the numbers, because the customers will be mad at me if they are not to their liking.

The next step is to take your appraisal card, the keys to the trade if the customer has one, and your worksheet to the sales manager. You may have to wait your turn, but with the customer signature your manager will know that you have a serious prospect. The manager will have the trade appraised and then it all begins. Management will sign your ACV (Actual Cash Value) card and you will return to your customer with a proposal to start your deal. This is called the "first pencil."

To help illustrate the process, I'll stay with the same fictitious set of numbers throughout this step. Let's say that the numbers your manager started you out with are $21,634 for the new car and $6,634 for the trade. Go back and present it this way. Have a smile on your face and use this word track, because words can make all the difference here. Say, "The selling price on our vehicle is $21,634 and my manager is willing to pay you $6,634 for your car, which would leave you $15,000 plus tax and license." *Now, zip your lip!*

He who speaks first loses. It's very important that once you serve up numbers to the customer, you wait for a response. Sometimes, I'll warn you, the silence is deafening; it seems like it takes ten minutes instead of 60 seconds. It's important that you are just silent now to let the customer respond. There are no exceptions to this rule.

Words are very important here, let me just take a second to caution you about using the word 'asking' during price presentation. If you were to say for instance we are 'asking' $21,634 for this vehicle, what have you already admitted? You've admitted that you're willing to come down and don't expect to get that price on the vehicle. For instance, if you were on a used car lot and a car had been marked down from $9,995 to $8,995, you should say, "The market value of this car is $9,995, but this week we have it advertised in the paper for $8,995, a savings of $1,000." If you say "We're asking $8,995," you've subtly implied that you'll take a lower price. To say, "I'm asking" doesn't make any sense at all. With an initial $1000 discount, you have little or no room to work with beyond the sale price of $8,995.

Overcoming Price Objections

Back to the deal. Now, it's show time. You've presented your numbers, and now it's the customer's turn. What is the customer going to say at this juncture? Well, you already know the answer to that. In some way shape or form, it'll boil down to, "It's what the not enough for my trade," or if the customer doesn't have a trade, "That's not enough discount," or "That's too much."

The way most salespeople deal with this situation is incorrect, and I hope you'll do it differently. What normally happens in the above scenario is you serve up the numbers and the customer returns with, "That's not enough for my trade; I think it's worth more than $6,634." The customary response by the salesperson is, "What did you have in mind?" The customer might say they think their car is worth $8,000, and then the salesperson responds by saying if they could get their boss to go to $8,000, for the trade, would you buy the new car now? What you've done in effect is hacked off $1,366 in gross without even attempting to justify the $6,634 offer.

In contrast, a better way to meet the objection, "not enough for my trade" is to respond **"Compared to what?"** Those are the first words out of my mouth because I realize I can't change their thinking if I don't understand their reasoning. I need to know their logic and how they arrived at the $8,000 figure.

To deal with an objection you must first, identify it, and second, solve it. Regardless of the type of objection (usually price), it's better to ask the question, "Compared to what?" They had to base their objection off of something, and what are their usual objections? These five objections will cover 99 percent of what you'll hear next:

a. Compared to what I owe on my trade.

b. Compared to another dealer's offer.

c. Compared to what I've seen in the paper or on the Internet.

d. Compared to the book price.

e. Compared to what my banker or credit union says.

I can't remember the last time I heard a new objection, and most salespeople have probably heard these five objections in their first month on the job. So we already know what customers are going to say when they walk in the door; that should give us confidence because all you have to do is load your gun with the right ammunition to counter the five objections above. My philosophy is that it's impossible for a part-time buyer to outmaneuver a full-time salesperson. Here's some ammo to deal with these objections one at a time.

Compared to what I owe on my trade

Use this explanation: "I appreciate the fact that you owe $7,500 dollars on your trade and my boss is only offering $6,634, but you do understand that what you owe has nothing to do with what your car is worth. I can certainly appreciate your situation, but usually when I have a customer in this predicament, one of the following conditions exist in their ownership: One, they drive more than 15,000 miles per year; two, they made very little or no down-payment; three, they used the longest term financing available; or four, they financed negative equity from their previous trade into their current loan."

Discover the reason for their situation and justify it to the customer, all the while explaining your dealership's stance in the trade evaluation. It's usually a case of excess yearly mileage when they are upside down on their trade. If you do a thorough *Step 5: Trade Evaluation,* you'll be able expand on the trade allowance justification.

Ask your customers if they'd rather owe too much money on a car they're looking forward to driving or one they are tired of driving. Try to get them to be reasonable about it. Does it work all the time? No. But if you can get them to open up on their trade situation, you can help explain your dealership's position and make them comfortable with the trade allowance. Express empathy if they are upside down on their trade, and tell them you can appreciate their situation, but what they owe on the car has nothing to do with its value.

If you need to expand on their situation a bit further, try this reasoning: the customer may be at a point of no return in regards to the ownership of their vehicle. If they have 70,000 miles or more on their vehicle, it's probably depreciating at a faster rate than what they're paying it down. Particularly if they drive more than 15,000 miles a year. As a vehicle approaches 100,000 miles, its marketability is significantly decreased. Additionally, the possibility of mechanical failure significantly increases. In conclusion, it will never be cheaper to trade than it is today. Our vehicle only goes up in price while your vehicle only goes down in price.

Compared to another dealer

Most salespeople handle this objection poorly. When you ask them "compared to what?" they'll say, "Compared to ABC Motors down the street; they'll give me $8,000 for my trade." Most salespeople make the mistake of responding, "If I can get my boss to match them will you agree to buy now?" Of course the customer responds, "Sure."

In that situation, you have to first ask yourself if the $8,000 figure is legitimate. The customer could be exaggerating; the salesperson at ABC Motors could be lying or stretching the truth. I don't know, and I won't assume that anyone is lying, but I have to at least consider the possibility.

Here is where you have to start asking questions to find out whether or not we're comparing apples to apples. Before I'll ever ask customers to commit to my dealership at the same price or trade allowance, I want to ask them the following: Ask them about the year, make & model, MSRP, and mileage. Ask them when the offer was made and by whom. Take them through the process and try to discover what's really going on.

Maybe they got an offer on a 2003 model and we're talking now about a 2003. Doesn't it make sense that the other dealer would have a lower price on an older model? Also, when you know the make and model of a car, you can find out the customer and/or dealer incentives. You can find these numbers out in *Automotive News* by looking at the back of the magazine at the listing of every rebate and incentive in the industry. I used to post that page in a manager's office so that salespeople were familiar with the incentives that our competition was currently offering. The other vehicle could also be a used car. What can they do to the asking price of a used car? Anything they want. They can set the margin to a point that they can over-allow more.

If, for instance, the customer is getting $8,000 on their trade on a Ford Taurus and I'm selling them a

Toyota Camry, I can look up the current rebates and incentives on the Taurus. If Taurus has a $1500 rebate, I can point out to the customer that it makes sense the other dealer offered more for their trade because of the rebates. Point out to them that they are comparing apples to oranges in this case. Maybe the Ford dealer is really giving them just $6,500 for their trade, not $8,000 because $1500 of it is rebate. Also, if ABC Motors had the rebate and I didn't, I'll ask the customers what they think a rebate does to the resale value of the car. The answer is, it brings it down because so much of resale value hinges on what it costs to replace a car.

If the MSRP is higher than the car you're selling, maybe the other dealer has a bigger margin on a more expensive car. If the other dealer is quoting on a $30,000 vehicle and you're quoting on one costing $20,000, it makes sense that the trade value your competition can over-allow is more due to the extra margin they have to work with. Explain that to the customer.

Ask about miles. Maybe the car ABC motors is selling is a demo with 6,000 miles on it, or maybe you're talking about used cars with different mileage.

When was the offer made? Was it six months ago? Is it still valid?

Who made the offer? Maybe it's just a salesperson talking. He or she could say "Maybe I can get you as much as $8000 for your trade." The customer, of course, hears that it's an $8,000 offer.

Another common scenario in which you'll have to take what the customer says with a grain of salt is when a customer announces he or she has been to three Chevy dealers and gotten prices on identical 2004 Monte Carlos. He says that if you give him the best price on the exact same car, they'll buy it from you. It happens all the time!

What do salespeople always do in this situation? I screwed this up for years before I understood the right way to handle the situation. We always ask, "What's the best price that you have received?" What are we really asking them to do here when we blurt out, "What's the best price?" We're asking them to lie to us, aren't we?

Everyone knows it's okay to lie to a car salesperson— Isn't it? I guess our culture reinforces the negative stereotypes about our profession so that even normally honest people think they are innocent when they stretch the truth in a car deal. Well, we don't want to put them in that position, so a better way to handle it is to take the high road and not ask that question. The method I'll describe is more professional and will help you sell more cars.

Here's what happens if customers exaggerate in this scenario: Let's say your cost, your dealer invoice on the car, is $20,000, and your customers have a real offer from a competitor for $20,500. They stretch the facts and tell you they have an offer for $19,500. You go to your boss and report the $19,500 offer. Your boss says the dealership can't sell it for that, and consequently you'll have to go back and walk your potential sale out of the store. The bad thing in this case is that no matter what you offer over your cost, they can't accept it or they will lose face and have to admit the fictitious $19,500 offer. The bottom line is you've given them no chance to buy a car from you.

Instead of this dead-end, how about if we did it this way? After stating they obtained prices from 3 dealerships already and will buy from you if you have the best price, you say, "Okay, I'll tell you what sir, I don't even want to know anything about the competing offer. First, I'd like to ask my manager to see what he can do, and I think once you evaluate our numbers, you'll choose to do business with us."

When the customer agrees to this proposition, take advantage of that opportunity and go for a mental commitment. Say to them, "If it turns out the numbers are agreeable and we can work out all the details to your satisfaction, can I tell my boss that you will buy now?" Get a mental commitment on the car and get them to sign a worksheet.

What happens when your boss pencils in $20,700? What happens is you actually have a chance to meet or beat the customer's legitimate best offer of $20,500. You're still in the game. I can't tell you how important this dynamic is. I did it wrong for 15 years and I never thought much about it. I know I lost a lot of deals and certainly an awful lot of gross by asking them to disclose that number.

Another scenario in this vein is that the salesperson at ABC Motors was less than honest with them about the $19,500 price. After you've gone through the process I just described and presented your price of $20,700, the customer says you're way off. You ask how close you are and press him until you get an idea of what they consider a fair price. The customer sticks with $19,500 and you and your manager know that he can't get it for that.

If I know the offer is fictitious, I need to find a way to get this buyer to come back later and deal with me. What I'll say is this, "Mr. Smith, I've enjoyed talking with you, but I've asked my boss and he doesn't see any way that someone can sell the car for that price, but if you can buy it for $19,500, run, don't walk, to that dealership. However, if you go back and talk to the salesperson who gave you that offer and they start to put you on the elevator and ask you to pay one dime more than $19,500, do yourself a favor—get up and walk out of there because they don't deserve to earn your business. Based on that price, we think that maybe you talked with a salesperson that wasn't completely truthful with you. If you want to call the competition right now and double check that price, you can use our private phone to see if that was a legitimate offer. If not, the salesperson lied to you. You wouldn't want to buy a car from someone who lied to you would you?"

What are you doing here is training your customers how to react when they talk to the competition. You also give the customer an out if they were the ones lying to you in the first place. If they were lying about the price, they can come back and save face by blaming it on the competing salesperson and you'll get another shot at their business.

When they try playing one dealer off another, do it this way. Don't ask the question, "What did they offer?" It's a dead end.

Compared to what I saw in the paper.

The customer will tell you they saw a car exactly like their trade advertised in the paper for $7,995, and in this scenario you'll have to point out to them that was a retail price. The used car dealer is 'asking' $7,995. Ask them what they think the dealer will really take for it? This time use the word **'asking.'** Let's say the customer responds with $7,500.

Say to them, "I'm not asking you to agree with me as much as I'm asking you to understand. What I feel I owe you is an explanation as to how my manager would come up with a number like $6,634. So, if you'll bear with me a minute, what I'd like to do is take you through the process of what takes place after we take in a used car on trade."

Explain to your customers that the first thing your dealership has to do with a trade is perform an inspection. That way they know if there is anything wrong with it. Based on that inspection, the dealership makes a decision as to whether or not they want to retail it. If they do, they put a warranty on it. Keep in mind that most dealerships only warranty cars with less than 75,000 miles. Then they do an extensive clean up on the car and have it detailed. The dealership will shampoo the carpets, buff the paint and steam-clean the engine. Your dealership may fix all the door dings, chips, etc. They may pay for a vendor to do miscellaneous repairs. Explain to your customers that the average reconditioning price is between $400-$600. Ask your boss for the exact number off of his financial statement. Find out what your dealership spends and tell the customers what it is and use actual numbers.

Here you can see the importance of having done a proper used car appraisal in *Step 5*. Mention to your customers any reconditioning needed on their trade and use that to justify your trade evaluation.

Let's play this out a littler further. After you've added the average $500 reconditioning expense to your trade offer of $6,634, you've got a price of $7,134, since the customer has already admitted that the market value is $7,500. Ask them if they think $366 is too much to make on a used car. If they say "yes," ask them what they think a fair profit should be on a used car? They may say, for instance, $200 sounds fair to them, and that's okay because now you've isolated a number and also logically justified your position. Now you're only $166 dollars apart, and you're nearing a closing offer.

What your customers really want to understand is the dealership logic on their trade value. Don't tell them that their car is worth $6,634 without telling them why your boss thinks so. Take them through your logic; tell them the truth and don't be apologetic about making money. Reasonable people understand that you need to make a commission and the dealership needs a profit.

Remember, trade allowance justification works a lot better if you properly went through the *Step 5* appraisal process and evaluated the trade based on its condition, not its book value.

Compared to the book value.

If I were to start selling cars all over again I wouldn't want to have access to a NADA or Bluebook.

Some stores allow salespeople to have these in their desks or in their pockets, but I think it will potentially cost you money if you use it at the wrong time. I don't want one, because you end up thinking it's the Bible and that it writes checks for cars. It doesn't. It's only a guide, and even in the front of the book it says, "The values in this guide assume a vehicle is clean. Appropriate deductions should be made for reconditioning costs incurred to put the vehicle in saleable condition. An exceptionally clean car, one that bears a guarantee, warranty or manufacturer's certification should bring a premium price."

This book isn't always accurate on many cars, and often you can buy a car for well under book. Also, the book values change every month. When did the customer last look at a current book? Is he or she aware that his or her trade might be on a used car lot for a few months and that before anyone buys it the Bluebook value will have declined? The bottom line is we are going to bid a car based on what we can get at auction or what another dealer will pay for it. They're worth what they're worth, and every dealership is going to pay about the same amount of money for them.

Ask them at this point if they got the average trade figure or the average retail figure out of the book. They might be confused about that number, or their banker may have given them the average retail number.

Often the banker or loan officer is the third baseman I've talked about. The banker or credit union hasn't even looked at or driven the car and doesn't have the whole picture. They pull out their trusty book and act like it's going to write a check for the used car. Sometimes I had to point out that if the trade were really worth $8,000, why would the banker only give them a loan for $6,000? The banker doesn't drive the car, take into consideration reconditioning, or on many occasions, even read the book correctly. Be skeptical about information coming third basemen. It may be inaccurate.

If I know what the buyer does for a living, and I may at this point, I'll try to put them in a place they understand. For instance, if they work at or own a shoe store or a lumber mill, I'll ask them if they pay retail when they buy their shoe or lumber inventory? Of course they don't. Well then they can probably see how my dealership can't pay retail for a used car. It's very effective to put customers in situations with which they can identify.

Here you need to show empathy and show that you care and justify your used car manager's position. Maybe you are overstocked in the used car inventory at this time or their model doesn't move very well. Justify your position. You owe the customer an explanation.

Step Down Method

People process and grasp written information better than oral information. At the closing I always have a legal pad and a blue or green pen. When nearing the close, I'll write the crucial numbers on the pad and turn them to the customer. For instance, I'll say in the above scenario, "If I can get my boss to go to $6950 on your trade, can we earn your business right now?" Then write the number $6950 on the pad and show it to them. Just show them the number, don't offer them pen and paper. What you've started here is the *Step Down Method,* and it works great in negotiation.

Ideally, I want to be in a position that every time I add money to the customers trade allowance or step down my offer, he or she wins. I want the step down increments to get smaller and smaller as we go back and forth. For instance on a trade allowance I might offer $7,050, then go to $7,100 then $7,125, then finally $7,135.

When the increments between numbers step down from 100, to 50, to 25, and even 10 dollars the customer begins to recognize that you've run out of negotiating room with your boss and are near the final number. When you do it this way eventually they'll spit out a number and it'll probably be a figure lower than the original $8,000 they wanted for their trade. The easiest price bump is the first one. Every time! That is, if you do it this way. When you step the numbers tighter and tighter to each other they should come to the conclusion that you've got the offer ground down to the minimum. Most sales-people don't have the guts to do it that way. You need courage to start stepping down to get the deal you need. With practice, it works quite well.

Solicit the best offer that you can.

After you've gone through the "compared to what" phase and the step down method, and the customer still won't budge, it's time to do some writing. Let's say the customer is stuck on $7500 for their trade and won't entertain another number. Or, they might be looking for a specific monthly payment number. Now, write down their offer on a worksheet and tell them you need them to do two things for you at this point. First, sign the worksheet that clearly describes the deal. Second, make out a check for $500 to the dealership. If you know they are planning on putting $2000 down on the loan, you should ask for that. In any event, ask for at least $500 as a sign of good faith partial payment.

They may ask why you need a check, and here's how you respond. The customer has everything to gain and nothing to lose when they write a check making an offer. The dealership is not in the business of keeping deposit checks. If you don't get together, they'll get their check back. Tell your customer, " It appears to me that you and my boss are $866 apart. You tell me. Am I better off bringing him your offer with or without a check?"

Getting a deposit gives you more leverage with your boss and shows the sincerity of the offer. Depending on your dealership policies you could take a check, a credit card, or even cash. Always put it in writing to make them feel more comfortable. You can also get a title to the trade as a deposit with the offer.

Some stores don't require a partial payment with an offer, but at others it's mandatory. It's sure a lot easier to execute a T.O., though, if you've got a deposit and the keys to the trade. At this point your sales manager will instruct you on how to work the deal. Maybe you can split the difference, or your manager may come up a little. I don't think that too many stores want to go back four or five times. I like to send the salesperson back maybe twice.

Some customers want to grind out six or seven rounds of this or they don't feel comfortable. That's fine with me if that's how they want to work the deal.

The Negotiate and Close step is easy and will go smoothly if you've invested the appropriate time and effort on steps one through six. Remember "Joe-Bag-A-Donuts?" There are two different ways to sell a car, "The Pro's way and Joe's way." The Pro spends 75 percent of his time on steps one through six and therefore only has to spend 25 percent on *Step 7*. Joe does it exactly opposite and spends 25 percent of his time on steps one through six and 75 percent of his time on *Step 7*. You see, Joe doesn't really know what he's doing. He doesn't have a plan or a strategy and wants to get to the reward of closing the sale before he's earned the right ask. The close is much tougher if you haven't taken the time to build value to justify price.

Additional Closing Techniques
Gas Mileage Comparison Worksheet.

This works great if you're selling a car that gets better gas mileage than the trade. For instance, the customers are trading an Expedition for a Taurus. It also works great with a payment buyer because it's easy to illustrate on monthly payments. Say you've offered a $325 per month payment and the customer wants $300. Try using the worksheet below to show them how they will save on monthly gas expenses for the new, more efficient vehicle and now can afford a $325 per month payment.

Say to them, "Here's something you might want to take into consideration. I can appreciate why you want to be at $300 per month, but I'm sure you based that off of what you normally spend on gas for the car you now have. However, based on my calculations, you'll save $50 per month on gas if you get the new Taurus." Show them the chart below.

GAS MILEAGE COMPARISON			
		OLD CAR	NEW CAR
Miles/Year		15,000	15,000
MPG	÷	15	25
Gallon/Year	=	1000	600
Cost per Gallon	x	$1.50	$1.50
Gas Cost/Year	=	$1500.00	$900.00

Savings per Year = $600.00
÷ 12 months
Saving per Month = $50.00
(See appendix for blank form)

If this technique only shows an advantage of $10 per month, it's worth using. As you can see in the example above, an increase of 10-mpg fuel efficiency gets you $50 in monthly gas savings based on 15,000 miles per year. It's very easy to plug in the numbers for any set of vehicles.

In addition, an older vehicle just costs more to operate on a daily basis, and the customer will save on any surprise repair expenses they will incur with an older vehicle. Mention that.

Total Cost Comparison

When you are in a situation in which the car you're selling holds better resale value than the competition's, regardless of the purchase price of the competing vehicle, point it out to the customer. Try to get people to look at the entire term of ownership rather than just the up-front purchase price of the car.

For instance, when I sold Honda Accords, there was a lot of competition from the Mazda 626. Both were quality cars that came in similar configurations and attracted the same sorts of buyers. Mazda didn't have the market share of the Accord and had recently marshaled an aggressive advertising program in order to gain ground on the Accord. Something I heard all the time from prospective buyers was that they liked both cars but were leaning toward the Mazda because it was $1,000 cheaper. The up-front sale price difference on the Mazda in comparison to the sales price on the Accord was all they could see.

I pointed out to them that if they drove the cars for four years before they sold them, they would be better off with the Accord. I would get the book and look up a four-year-old Mazda 626 and see what its current value was. Using typical mileage and the base figure in the book, I found that the four-year-old 626 was vlaued at $2,000 less than a similarly equipped four-year-old Accord.

One could conclude from this comparison that the Mazda depreciated more in four years than the Accord. So, which car really costs more to own? You could also break it down into monthly depreciation by dividing total depreciation by the number of months of anticipated ownership. Your dealerships have comparison guides for competing models and you should school yourself on these details. Get the customer to consider the total term of ownership because that's the only way you can logically discover the real cost of ownership.

Delay Payments for 45 Days.

Here's another closing situation that's pretty common. Say a customer wants a $300 dollar per month payment and your boss needs a $325 per month payment. By the way, $25 per month on the average car deal is about $1,250 on the total deal, and many dealerships routinely walk this buyer if they have this much separation. People often want a payment schedule based on a car they bought 4 years ago and expect to keep their new payments the same, even though the new model has risen in price. It's not logical, but we battle with this mindset every day. If you are separated on payments like this, tell your customers you think you might know a way that you can justify the new $325 payment

I've found that many, many people come to buy a car just before their next car payment is due. For instance, if today is October 20th and they have a payment due this week. Tell them you think you can get your finance manager to set their first payment to come due in 45 days. This is a common practice at most dealerships.

Explain to them the next two payments they were expecting to pay on their old car won't need to be paid. Plus, the two weeks additional is equivalent to half of a payment. This gives them an extra $750 to play with that they would have normally budgeted for payments. That's today's payment, next month's, and part of the following month's payment. If you subtract the $325 payment they didn't have to make in October from $750, they'll have an additional $425 in their pocket they didn't normally have.

Now, take the $425 and divide by the $25 a month that you are apart with the customer and you'll get 17 months before their budget feels any pinch because of the change in payment. See the chart below and write it out for the customer.

Payment Schedule		
	Old Car	New Car
10/20	$300	$0
11/20	$300	$0
12/05	$150	$325
Total	$750	$325

$425 is the difference.
Divided by the payment difference of $25 equals 17 months. $150 is 1/2 of payment because 11/20 to 12/05 is only 2 weeks.

For many people who are expecting a routine raise or job promotion, it's easy to envision affording an extra $25 per month 17 months down the road. On top of that, they will not have incurred any surprise expenses or repairs on an older vehicle during these 17 months. This approach worked for me all the time, and I would try it long before my customers were ready to walk.

Rebate/Equity close

For example, the customer wants $400 a month payment, and we need $450 a month. This is another situation that may appear unworkable, and a decision is made to walk the customer. Let's reconsider. Say that the numbers break down like this:

Sale price = $40,000 (includes $2000 customer rebate)

Trade allowance = $15,000

Trade difference = $25,000 (monthly payments of $450)

The hill appears to be too big to climb, but if I get creative I can close the deal. Let's have the customer fill out a credit application and see if we can't find a way to put this deal together. Upon review of the application we see the following:

	Balance	Monthly Payment
Marshal Fields	$200	$20
Nordstrom's	$300	$30
VISA	$500	$50
MasterCard	$1,000	$100
Total	$2,000	$200

Now demonstrate the following and change the numbers to this:

Sale price   = $42,000

(customer keeps $2000 rebate and applies   to high-interest credit card bills)

Trade allowance = $15,000

Trade difference = $27,000 ($490 monthly payment)

When we analyze this scenario, we see that the amount financed rose $2,000 and the customer's payments will increase to approximately $490 per month. However, tell the customer to use the $2,000 rebate to pay off his or her high-interest credit cards, and by doing that he or she will save themselves $200 per month in payments. Now the car payment is $90 more than he or she wanted, but his or her overall short-term budget will be $110 less after the high-interest credit cards are paid off.

This could also work with a customer that has a lot of equity in his or her trade but no available rebate. Talk to your F&I manager as to whether or not a lender would let them pull out some equity to eliminate credit card debt.

"What's your best price?"

One of the most difficult situations that salespeople face on a regular basis is when a customer wants our price, but isn't willing to commit to buy now. I don't want to give the customer my best price unless they're willing to buy now, because then the customer has no reason to come back. Additionally, I would be giving them a shopping ticket. Whenever I was in this situation I explained like this.

I said, "The best price is the one I can get my manager to approve. Price is a function of management and I have nothing to do with that decision. I'm sure that there are decisions that you can't make at your job and price is one that I can't make at mine. Let me explain. If I walk into my boss' office right now and say that I have a customer that wants our best price, he is going to ask me two questions. Have they selected and driven a car in stock? And, if they like the price, are they prepared to make a decision right now? If I say no to either one of these questions he won't give me a price.

"Now before you get excited, let me explain why. My manager wants to earn your business and understands that by giving you a price, he risks losing your business. When we give a price, it makes it too easy for another dealership to beat us by $50. In effect, we would be giving an advantage to our competition and I'm sure you can understand why we wouldn't want to do that.

"I want to think about it."

When faced with this objection, here's a good word track to try: "I can appreciate the fact that you feel the need to think about it, because this is a major decision. At times in my life when I hesitated to make a major decision, each and every time, I recognized that there was something that wasn't quite right. In your case, what would that be?"

Hopefully, the customer will then state the final objection or concern and allow you to close the deal.

Things to Remember:

- Get a written Mental Commitment.
- Don't use the word "asking."
- Numbers are a function of management.
- When you present your offer—Shut Up!
- Words are important at closing. Learn your word tracks.
- The five most common price objections when we say "compared to what."

a) Compared to what I owe on my trade.

b) Compared to another dealer's offer.

c) Compared to what I've seen in the paper.

d) Compared to the book price.

e) Compared to what my banker or credit union says.

- "Keep that number to yourself."
- Shrink price increments in the Step Down Method.
- Additional closing techniques and word tracks to help overcome objections.

a) Gas mileage comparison

b) Total cost comparison

c) Delay initial payments

d) Rebate/Equity close

e) "What's your best price?"

f) "I want to think about it."

Aftermarket and Turn Over

Goals:

- Sell after-market options.
- 100% T.O. to Sales Manager on every *up*.
- 100% T.O. to Business Manager (F&I) at point of sale.

In this step, let's talk about presenting after-market options and turning over the customer to the Sales Manager and the Business Manager. This is a step that needs to be completed in order to inform the customer of add-on options, to finalize or save the deal with your manager, and to arrange for financing and the sale of products sold by your finance department.

Aftermarket

Aftermarket is any available feature or option that is not currently on the vehicle as it sits on the lot. For instance, rust proofing, undercoating, paint sealant, fabric protection, bug deflectors, bumpers, hitches, CD changers, stripe packages, graphics packages, power sunroof, pop-up sunroof, etc.

Some stores have an after-market manager who specializes in selling these options, but in most cases, the salespeople are the ones who sell them. The number one thing to remember on this is to not bring up the availability of an after-market option until after you've consummated the deal. We've agreed to sell, they've agreed to buy. After the numbers have been set in stone and there is absolute, mutual agreement, then, and only then, talk about after-market options. Why is that? Because if you start talking about these extras before the deal is complete, customers will just want them thrown in with the deal. Make it clear that these options are in addition to the agreed upon price.

However, if the customer were to say they wouldn't buy this truck without a bed-liner, then of course write that into the structure of the deal. That's because they brought it up, not because I started throwing out ideas. If I bring up after-market options before the deal is finalized, all it's going to do is increase the overall price and make the vehicle harder to sell.

The really neat thing about after-market sales is that customers typically won't try to negotiate the price of options after the sale. When looking at the after-market book or price list they'll pay the price they see in the book. If the CD changer is listed at $899, they typically won't try to negotiate the price down to $650. They'll pay the price they see on paper.

Some dealerships have sleek after-market books showing pictures of all the accessories. There are so many things available in after-market and there's money to be made selling them. We lose a lot of opportunity for additional gross because we don't do a good job of presenting these options. Sometimes you might take a minimum commission on a deal and double it just due to the profit you can make in after-market options. It can take a below average car deal and make it an above average deal and put extra money in your pocket.

100% TurnOver (T.O.) to the Sales Manager

Turnover (T.O.)—that's what you need to do when you reach an impasse with a prospect. Your Sales Manager is your best friend in the business and is there to help you succeed. They make their living off your success and have a vital self-interest in helping you prosper. If for whatever reason the prospect is not buying that day, or maybe has an objection you don't feel you're able to handle, then you need to turn it over to a manager. A good word track to help properly handle a T.O. might be something like, "Folks, before you leave, I just want to check on one thing with my boss. I want to ask him a question."

Now when you get to your boss, and you have to do this quickly, give him or her the *Reader's Digest* version of the transaction. It might go something like this: "Boss, here's where I'm at. He said this, she said that, we demoed the car, they liked the ride, and they're also shopping at ABC motors down the road." Give your boss a lay of the land; he or she doesn't need to know the *War and Peace* version. By giving your manager this information, he or she can make a decision as to the proper course of action to take.

You should be aware that a decision for a customer to walk off the dealership is a management decision, not a salesperson's decision. I know some of your stores aren't strict on T.O., but if they are, you'll know it quickly. I believe that after 3 strikes, you're out, and I don't care how good you are. First strike was a warning, second was a slap on the wrist, and the third you're out the door.

As a manager I make my living off the sale of cars here, too; if you don't T.O., you're messing with my income, and I'll take offense to that. I was strict about it, and I couldn't understand why a salesperson wouldn't T.O., because he or she had everything to gain and nothing to lose by turning it over to the manager. Two heads are better than one, and sometimes your manager will say just the right thing to make the difference. Sometimes the manager can say the exact same thing you just said and the customer might respond, "Okay, I'll buy it." Who knows? It's always worth a try.

Your manager knows the inventory and what cars are coming in. He or she has dealt with these objections a thousand times. He is also the best closer in the store, or he probably wouldn't be the manager. With all these things working in your favor, it's foolish not to T.O. If your store doesn't require it, I'd still suggest you utilize a manager that's open to going out and talking to a customer. You'll sell more cars.

When I was the manager, I'd try to close the sale if I thought it was an objection I could deal with and possibly overcome. If I didn't feel I could close that deal, I'd thank them for coming to the store and extend our gratitude. Often a T.O. would begin like this, "Mr. and Mrs. Smith, my name is Mike Radosevich—everybody calls me Radar—I'm the manager of the store. I just want to thank you for coming in and giving us an opportunity to show our vehicles. Did Bill do a good job with you and answer all of your questions? Well, great, I just want to thank you once again. I'll give you one of my business cards so that in the event that you come in again and Bill isn't here, please feel free to ask for me. My office is open anytime."

What about customers who won't stick around to talk with a manager? Those things happen. The toughest T.O. is when you're on the lot and you can't get them in the door. If they won't drive the car, it's hard to get them in for a T.O. I used to say, "Come on in, I'll get you a brochure or some information that might be valuable to you," and then see if my manager could help. You have everything to gain and nothing to lose by a T.O., and once again you're extending another friendly hand to a prospect, which will only benefit you in the long run.

100% T.O. to a Business Manager (F&I) at Point of Sale.

F&I stands for Finance and Insurance. They are the business managers and those who do all of the paperwork. There are absolutely, positively, no exceptions for missing a T.O. with these people. Point of Sale means when the deal is done and all the numbers have been agreed upon.

Lets say, for instance, the customer comes in, you wait on them, demo the car, write the deal up and it's a done deal, they agree and we agree to sell for 20 grand. You don't have the car in stock, it's a dealer trade or ordered from the factory and won't be in for a month. Now, before that customer leaves the dealership, you need to pass him to an F&I Manager.

We want to secure the financing on the deal, because when you control the financing on the car deal you control the deal. The last thing you want is to get a third baseman involved. By that I mean an inexperienced banker or bystander who wants to pull out a *NADA* or *Kelly Bluebook* and quote trade-in prices. That's what happens when you cut them loose and they consult with a third baseman. It could be a banker, Uncle Joe, or anyone who says, "I'll show you how to buy a car." Instead, I want them meeting with our business or finance department and putting down a deposit on the car, with total numbers written up and them filling out a credit application.

If they plan on using their own bank or credit union then just say, "Okay, I'm going to introduce you to my business manager, and he'll give you the total numbers with tax and license so you know what to give to your banker."

When the customer is in finance, the business manager will still have a good shot at securing the financing. Maybe we can save him or her some money. In most cases we can. Your dealership probably has 10-15 lenders, and they shop for the best rates, the best terms. The business manager will interview the buyer and find out what lending instrument works best for his or her individual circumstances.

When we secure financing, we also have the chance to offer an extended warranty. One of the things I always did at F&I turn over was throw in a plug about extended warranties. I would tell them about Jeff in finance that runs the extended warranty department and strongly suggest they talk to him. Or I'd introduce them to Jeff, and then before I left I'd say, "Jeff, be sure to explain the available extended warranty." He used to just love me for it. He'd bring it up in sales meetings all the time, because my customers bought more extended warranties than any other salesperson.

I had a high percentage of warranty sales because I planted the seed and I endorsed it. If I've earned their trust by selling them a car, I also want to sell them a warranty. I buy warranties myself. I bought one on my son's SUV, and it cost $1,800. I fully believe in them. If someone drives only 12,000 miles a year and owns the car for three years, he or she probably isn't going to buy an extended warranty, but they are transferable to the next buyer, which really increases the resale value of the car. There are a lot of benefits in purchasing an extended warranty. Ultimately what it does is protect the customer. It also protects the salesperson and the dealership against an unhappy customer.

Let's face it—things happen to cars. They sometimes break down. I don't want to see one of my customers coming into service needing a $4,000 repair without an extended warranty. It's a bad reflection on me, but it can happen. Tell them you don't buy life insurance with the hopes of using it, and you don't buy car insurance hoping you need it. Paying $20 to $25 a month is a lot cheaper than pulling three or four grand out of your pocket.

Take this T.O. seriously, because the second best friend you can have in the dealership is the business manager. Building a relationship based on trust with the business manager can help you get your deals through. I used to make some deals that other salespeople couldn't. I did a big job for my business manager, and he had favors sitting in the wings for me. Many times a finance manager is taught to sandwich a marginal deal between two "A" paper deals, and I know I got my share of the marginal deals approved. Why? Because I made him more money than any other salesperson and that was his way of saying thanks.

Once again, it is developing relationships with all of the people you work with, from the mechanics and the office staff to the Sales and Finance managers. If you respect what they do with their time, they'll respect what you do with yours. Mutual respect is necessary so there won't be as many walls built between different departments. With a team the atmosphere that springs from trust and appreciation, there's no telling what you can accomplish.

Things to Remember:

- Don't sell after-market options until after you have consummated a deal.

- The Sales Manager is your best friend.

- The Business/Finance Manager is your second best friend.

Delivery

Goals:

- Thoroughly fill out the Get-Ready or Due Bill to Schedule Delivery.
- Prepare Owner's packets well in advance.
- Tailor your delivery process to the Customer Satisfaction Survey (CSI).
- Promote yourself and be accessible.

Generate a Get-Ready Form and Schedule Delivery

Once you've sold a car, generate a Get-Ready/Due Bill form. You're ready for delivery now, and the Get-Ready form asks for information like the VIN or serial number, customer's name, mileage, delivery time and date, etc. Every dealership has its own method. Be sure to be thorough when filling out the form.

When the service department asked me the time of delivery, I always subtracted one hour. It's a white lie, but you'll need that extra hour to double-check all the delivery details. Trust me, if your customer is coming in at five o'clock, put four o'clock on your Get-Ready form. I want that one-hour buffer if something goes wrong in service when they're prepping the new car. As the salesperson, it's your responsibility to make sure everything is just right on delivery. Be sure to prepare the Owner's Packet well in advance.

Next, depending on the policy of your dealership be sure to **verify and schedule the delivery with F&I** or your business manager. Some of you have sign-up sheets outside the finance office. Be sure you have all of your paper work done and forms filled out properly when you go to F&I. If you don't do this, you'll create problems in F&I, and scheduling delivery will be a hassle for everyone. Get all the numbers and details that are required. It's your job. The delivery process will go much more smoothly if you do it right the first time.

Check on the status of the vehicle. Don't go back to bother anyone, but about an hour before the scheduled delivery, just peek into service to see if the process has begun for delivery. All of you have a staging area either on the show floor or on the lot. Go check it, because if service is backed up, you may need to call your customer and reschedule. There's nothing worse than customers who've eagerly anticipated owning a new car having to stand around and wait because of a delay in the clean-up department. It should be an exciting time for them, and you should realize this and foster that excitement.

Salesperson's Final Inspection

At some point the vehicle will be brought up, and you should make a Salesperson's Final Inspection. Walk around and make sure there are no light exterior scratches or dust and smudges on the dash. Maybe a tech got grease on the floor at the last minute. You'll want to make sure you have nothing to apologize for when the customer takes delivery. I bring a towel and some glass cleaner because I want every vehicle "in the crate," "in the wrapper," "brand new." No surprises! Clean the mirrors. Buff it if necessary. Make it perfect!

Pull the keys and lock the doors if it's okay with your dealership. You don't want anyone getting in to the vehicle and messing it up at this point. Another customer or salesperson might not know that it's a sold vehicle and get inside. Who knows?

When the customer comes in for delivery, the first thing I do is say to them, "Before you take delivery and sign out on your vehicle, I want you to inspect the car and make sure that it is exactly what you expected." Get the customer's final approval.

The Owner's Packet

The owner's packet contains the Owner's Manual, Warranty Book, Maintenance Schedule, Bird Dog reminder (Referral request), and Key Codes on two of your business cards.

Try to get the delivery, or owner's, packets ready as far in advance as possible, because you don't want to be scrambling at the last minute. With some advance planning you can deliver multiple vehicles on the same day without unnecessary pressure. I had one day when I delivered eight cars, and you need to be organized if you're going to do that.

The exact order in which you complete the following delivery steps will be dictated by the availability of the Business Manager. As soon as you get the customer's final approval, get them to your Business Manager. If the Business manager is not available, you can review the owner's packet, one item at a time. When the customer is with the business manager, offer to assist in the transfer of personal belongings, plates, sticker, etc., while they sign out. An additional nice touch would be to pre-set the radio stations in the new car to the same ones stored in their trade. Don't let your customer sit around and wait, and don't do something else, like take an *up,* for instance, when the customer is in the business office. It's rude, and I've seen it happen many times.

Use the owner's packet to keep the customer busy if the F&I or business office is unavailable. Bring him or her into your office and explain each item. If he or she doesn't have many questions, this process should take approximately ten minutes, but take as long as he or she needs. You can always interrupt your explanation of the packet if F&I becomes available, then return to it later.

Explain the Owner's Packet One Item at a Time

Here are some word tracks that may be useful.

Owner's Manual: "This is the Owner's Manual. It will tell you everything you need to know about your vehicle. So if there's anything you forget, it will be a good point of reference for you."

Show them the index and explain what it covers. Point out where to find interesting features or subtle benefits.

Warranty Book: "This is the Warranty Book. It explains the manufacturer's warranty in detail. The basic warranty is ___years or ___ miles with___ deductible. The emissions warranty is ___ years or ___ miles. The power train warranty is ___ years or ___ miles."

Detail the terms and conditions of each part and make sure they understand them.

The Maintenance Schedule: "This is the manufacturer's suggested maintenance schedule. You need to follow this to be in compliance with their requirements. It would also be beneficial for you to service your vehicle here so there will always be a hard copy file of your service history. It could come in handy in the event of any questionable warranty claims."

Many dealerships have prepared a schedule that's compliant with the manufacturer's guidelines. They may have a menu pricing of services. Go over the basics.

Bird Dog Reminder: (Only in states where legal) "This is a Bird Dog Reminder. In the event you have a friend, relative, neighbor, or business acquaintance that is interested in a new or used vehicle, please give them my card. If your referral results in a sale, the dealership authorizes me to send you a $___ referral fee."

See the sample in the final chapter. (Sample forms)

Key Codes/Business Cards: Explain to them that the key codes will allow a locksmith to cut them another set of keys without having to have a copy of the key (non-diod keys only). Normally, customers might throw away or lose your business card, but if you write the key codes on the back of your card, they'll hang on to it. They might throw away your card, but they won't throw away their key codes. It helps them remember you.

Customer Satisfaction Surveys

Your ability to properly deliver a vehicle will have everything to do with your own personal CSI (Customer Satisfaction Index). Study the survey and tailor your delivery presentation to the items on the survey. Every time you deliver a new car, the customer will be sent a survey from the manufacturer asking them to evaluate your performance and that of the dealership based on their buying experience.

It is in your best interest to have the highest CSI that you can, because that will ensure repeat and referral business. That survey is going to ask the customer questions about their satisfaction level with you as a salesperson and the dealership in general. The manufacturer will use a scale that depicts the customer's level of satisfaction.

This is your report card and has an awful lot to do with your future success in this business. Listen to what your customers are telling you. Depending on the manufacturer, the survey will ask the customer to rate you on any or all of the following areas of the sales and delivery process:

- Ease of doing business
- Handling of vehicle purchased
- Courtesy
- Sincerity
- Honesty
- Concern for customer needs
- Greeting
- Knowledge of manufacturer's products
- Knowledge of competitive products
- Knowledge of service required
- General appearance
- Features and benefits
- Knowledge of warranty
- Delivery of vehicle was convenient
- Delivered with all promised features
- Time spent with customer
- Explanation of vehicle control
- Exterior clean and undamaged
- Interior clean and undamaged
- Explanation of owners manual
- Explanation of required maintenance
- Introduction to service department
- Follow-up

The manufacturer compiles the totals and they report the individual and dealer CSI results every month. You'll most likely get yearly and quarterly ratings that report your own personal CSI. Some of you will be on a four-point scale, which varies from manufacturer to manufacturer. For instance, a score of "4" would be perfect for some of you. Others are on a 100 point scale, in which case "100" would be perfect. A perfect score means you're completely satisfying your customer in every way, every time you sell a car.

You'll be ranked in your district, and if you want a high ranking it will come down to two things: Number one, the manner in which you sold a car, and number two, the manner in which you delivered it. Understand the delivery procedure and develop your own procedure that satisfies every question on the survey. Upon receipt of your individual totals, take some time to evaluate your performance and make necessary changes in your sales/delivery process.

Review the Satisfaction Survey with the Customer at Delivery

Tell your customers they will be receiving a survey from the manufacturer and stress how important it is for them to give you a "Completely Satisfied" score on the survey. Tell them you would appreciate it if they would take a few short minutes to fill it out and send it back to the manufacturer. Urge customers to call you when they receive the survey if they cannot honestly answer every question as "Completely Satisfied." Tell them it's your report card, and ask them for the personal favor of filling it out. To show them what the survey looks like, I laminated one that was filled out "Completely Satisfied," and I quickly went over the items on it. I wanted to demonstrate my commitment to their satisfaction, and sometimes I'd make a joke about it, telling them if they didn't understand a question to call me because I knew all the right answers. Or, if they didn't have the time to fill it out, just send it to me and I'd fill it out for them.

Most salespeople underestimate the importance of the survey and don't ask customers to fill it out. Understand this: seeing as how we live in a negative world, unhappy and disgruntled customers will have a tendency to fill out the survey. On the other hand, most happy and satisfied customers won't feel the need to express their feelings. By asking your customers to take the time to fill out the survey, the ones that you add will typically be good ones. I got 65 percent to 70 percent return rate on my surveys because I asked for the personal favor, and as a result, my CSI increased. You're never going to be perfect, but you can strive to be. To keep your CSI high you'll need all the positive responses you can get to offset any negative surveys.

Service Walk

Show them the facilities and explain the procedures when they need to get service. Introduce them to service personnel if possible. Each dealership has different policies. Some manufacturer surveys ask if the customer was introduced to the service department. Find a way to cover this at your dealership. I often deliver cars from 6:00 p.m. to 9:00 p.m., when the service department is closed, so I put pictures of the service writers and managers on the wall and show customers who to talk to when they needed help.

Feature Operations

Some customers may object to having to go through every facet of the operation of all features, but go ahead and give them the best presentation you can. The only time I would short cut that would be if the new car was the same model as the old car and the features were the same. Address small features that may have changed since the last model or little known features. If needed, use the list below for some ideas on what to present to your customer.

Checklist of Vehicle Features
- Anti-lock brakes
- Instrument panel warning lights and gauges
- Driver controls (tilt, cruise, wipers, headlights, mirrors, locks, windows, etc.)
- Heater, ventilation, air-conditioning
- Radio and clock settings
- Fuse block location
- Seat belts, air bags, safety features
- Seat adjustments
- Hood latch and location of fluid checks and fills
- Spare tire and jack location and instructions
- Anything else, especially new or little known features.

Open the hood and show where the fluids go. Show your customers how to check the oil, brake, transmission, radiator, power steering, and window washer fluids. Show them the fuse block and how it works. Show them the trunk and how the jack and spare come out. Show them all the little things they may not know and then ask if they have any questions. Many of these things you may have touched on when you demo-ed the car, but you should feel obligated to educate your customer about all feature operations on their new vehicle.

Use the "Delivery Checklist" if necessary. Tell them that if they have any questions or problems to please call. Thank them for their business and tell them that you will be checking with them periodically to make sure they're happy with their new car.

Promote Yourself at Delivery

The best time to promote yourself and let the customer know you'll be there for them in the future is at delivery. You're in business for yourself and this is the best time to spread the word. Word of mouth is very powerful, and you need to prove your commitment to the buyer. I put my home number and cell number on my cards, in addition to the store numbers. Pagers are extremely inexpensive, and they're worth while, it because a customer who has a question deserves prompt attention. It'll save you a lot of money in split deals and increase customer satisfaction and reduce frustration. Most salespeople don't put their personal phone numbers on their card, and it always impressed my customers that I was willing to make the commitment to service their needs outside of my regularly scheduled hours.

I went to a local printer and got a rubber stamp of my schedule to stamp the back of my business cards so customers would know when I was scheduled to be in the store. It's only a few bucks, and I could just tell customers that my schedule was on the back of my card. If they needed to reach me—they could call my cell or pager and if I couldn't meet them I'd set them up with the right person. You'll also have fewer split commission deals if you are willing to do this.

Another great thing is to take advantage of specialty advertising. I have given all my customers a key chain with the dealership name and my name and numbers on it. I have used lots of things, little knives, lights, hats, pens, or key fobs in different colors. I have used refrigerator magnets with "bird dog" reminders, like "Turn this into real money—ask me how." Use any personal marketing ideas to keep your name out there. These things aren't expensive and average only about $5 per customer, plus they're tax deductible. I also have my own personalized birthday cards and thank-you cards and have found them to be good investments in my future, because these products keep my name in front of the customers.

Things to Remember:
- Get-Ready form and schedule delivery
- Salesperson's final inspection
- Owner's Packet
- Owner's Manual
- Warranty Book
- Maintenance Schedule
- Bird-dog reminder
- Key Codes on two of your business cards (one for each driver)
- Explain Customer Satisfaction Survey (CSI)
- Service Walk
- Promote yourself and be accessible
- Make commitment to customer to follow-up after delivery

Delivery Check List

Customer Name: _____

Customer Phone Number: _____

Vehicle Purchased: _____

Date of Delivery:_____ Stock #: _____

- ❑ Explained Owner's Manual
- ❑ Explained Warranty Coverage
- ❑ Explained Maintenance Requirements
- ❑ Familiarized Customer with Service Department
- ❑ Customer was Introduced to Service Personnel
- ❑ Salesperson Demonstrated all Features on Vehicle
- ❑ Customer was given Delivery Checklist
- ❑ Customer was Introduced to Sales Manager
- ❑ Vehicle Interior and Exterior Clean and Undamaged
- ❑ Customer Informed of Customer Survey

CUSTOMER SIGNATURE   SALESPERSON SIGNATURE

Notes:

Prospect and Follow-Up

Goals:

- Use your Prospect Log to follow-up daily.
- Do a self-evaluation weekly.
- Make a list of potential customers—everyone you know.
- Write a "New Career Letter" (if applicable).
- Practice a customer follow-up schedule.
- Build a network that gets you referrals.

Prospect Log

A prospect log is an invaluable tool. Every time I got an *up* I'd fill out the prospect log, and at the end of every week I'd do a self-evaluation. I did my self-evaluation faithfully every Monday morning. Now, if you take the time to do this, you'll identify your weaknesses and how to correct them. Few salespeople do this, but if they did they would set themselves apart from the pack and really increase their success.

PROSPECT LOG

DATE	PROSPECT NAME	PHONE	VEHICLE/INTEREST	TRADE-IN	D	W	S	L	COMMENTS

The prospect log is pretty straightforward. After each *up* go and record the information on this chart. Record date, prospect name, phone, vehicle they were interested in, and their trade vehicle. The DWSL columns stand for:

D = **Demo-ed**. Did you demo the car, yes or no? (check the box)

W = **Write-up.** Did you get a verbal/mental commitment to buy now?

S = **Sold.** Did you secure the financial commitment and agree on figures?

L = **Last Step Completed**. What was the last step you completed during the sales process (steps 1-7)?

When you look at the Last Step Completed column over a period of time, you may see a pattern developing. If you continually get stuck in the same place, it might open your eyes to your problems. A lot of disappointment comes when you aren't selling enough cars and you don't know why. If you are frustrated with selling cars but keep a diligent and faithful record of your prospect log, it can cue you into the help you need. Your log will show which steps you need to work on and where you're going wrong. In the L column write down the last sales step you were on when the customer left the dealership. Analyze the patterns you may see emerge. It makes sense that if you are continually getting stuck on one step, there must be a failure lying somewhere prior to that. Go back and review these steps to identify your weaknesses.

The first thing Monday morning I draw a line through the bottom column and begin calculating my totals for the previous week. The first total is how many *ups* I took for the week. Second was how many of those *ups* I turned into demos. Then, how many demos did I write-up, and finally, how many write-ups did I sell?

Self-Evaluation

Here's a Self-Evaluation based on some sample numbers taken from a Prospect Log. The columns have been totaled for a week. Notice there were 15 *ups*, ten demos, five write-ups and two sold. There were ten demos, which were 67 percent of the *ups*, and the last steps were 1, 2, and the first half of step 3. In the write-up column there were 5 write-ups, which were 50 percent of the demos, and the last steps were the last half of steps 3, 4, 5, and 6. In the sold column there were two cars sold, which were 40 percent of the write-ups, and the last step mentioned was of course step 7. Take note of the goal percentages of 80 percent demo, 60 percent write-ups and 60 percent sold, because I'll explain them later.

SELF EVALUATION

What can you conclude from this self-evaluation? Notice that this sample has a 67 percent rate for demos and the goal is 80 percent. This salesperson must be having problems in one of the first three steps, either *Meet & Greet, Qualify,* or *Interior Feature/Benefit* presentation.

	NUMBER	%	GOAL	STEPS
UPS	15			
DEMOS	10	67	80%	1,2, 1/2, 3
WRITE-UPS	5	50	60%	1/2, 3, 4, 5, 6
SOLD	2	40	60%	7

PLAN OF ACTION:

Typically, most of the problems for beginning car salespeople rest in *Step 2: Qualify,* because if you can't push enough hot buttons or identify enough dominant buying motives to give that customer the desire to want a demo ride, then you're failing somewhere within the steps. Go back and make sure that you are asking all 18 qualify questions and ask for the three most important features the customer is looking for in a new vehicle.

If you know what step you are on and the step that comes next, you can succeed in this business. What you're trying to do is break the sales process down in a logical and systematic fashion so that you can discover what step you need to improve. Maybe it's *Step 3* and your product knowledge is weak, or perhaps your interior feature/benefit presentation is inefficient and clumsy.

In the sample above, write-ups were five out of ten, which is 50 percent of the demos in the sample. My goal is 60 percent, so I can conclude I need improvement in *Step 3,4,5 or 6.* Usually it's a lack of product knowledge and not asking enough open-ended questions or not tailoring your presentation towards the wants and needs of the customer.

In the above sample, the sold to write-up ratio was 40 percent, which indicates that *Step 7 Negotiate and Close* still needs work.

Why do these goal percentages in the table above mean so much? They reflect what you'll need to do to achieve a 25 percent closing ratio. Let's look at it in depth and translate the monthly goals in the sample into the real world. First of all, you should have 60 *ups* a month—that's fewer than three a day and you need that many to reach your goals. You should demo 80 percent of that 60 and end up with 48 demos. When you write up 60 percent of those 48 demos, you'll be left with 28 write-ups. Ideally, you'll sell 60 percent of the write-ups, which leaves you with 17 car deals out of 60 *ups.* Now keep in mind that you never deliver all the cars you sell, because people back out or financing falls through. You may lose a couple of deals due to this sort of problem. That still leaves you with 15 sold and delivered cars and 25 percent of the 60 *ups* you took for the month. Initially, this is where I would want your closing ratio to be. Selling 25 percent of your *ups* is a worthy goal. As you become more proficient in the sales process, your sales will increase even if your *ups* don't.

MONTHLY GOALS

You can't eat an elephant in one bite, but you can eat an elephant, one bite at a time. Break your goals down to daily, weekly, and monthly values. This way you're more likely to accomplish whatever ultimate goals you set out for yourself.

	NUMBER	%
Ups	60	
Demos	48	80%
Write-ups	28	60%
Sold	17	60%
Delivered	15	

Set small daily goals for yourself. Sixty *ups* a month is less than three *ups* a day. If you fall behind one day and only get two, make up for it the next day and get four. Take 15 *ups* a week and so on. Many times salespeople get to the end of the month with only eight cars sold and wonder why. Most of the time they haven't checked their Prospect Log all month, and when they do they find they've only taken 40 *ups*. No big surprise to me! And it shouldn't be to you either.

If you do this process every week and honestly and accurately record the numbers, I can tell you which step in the sales process you were not completing as thoroughly as you need to. You could call or fax them to me even if you were out of state and I could tell you what's wrong. It's a simple process, and I hope you do it because it will help you reduce frustration and sell more cars. Write it down and focus on weaknesses!

You should also do a post-mortem after every deal. Where did you get stuck? What did they say? What objections couldn't you overcome? Hindsight is 20/20, and it's easier to analyze and isolate your problems with a little time to reflect.

Prospecting

This is a way to find car deals that don't just walk in the door. You should be shaking the bushes out there all the time. New salespeople, or those who've changed jobs or dealerships, should get a letter out to everyone they know. Tell them where you work and would love to hear from them. In the back of the book I have a sample letter that's worked very well for my students. Use it!

Don't prejudge the list you create. You never know who may be looking for a car, and they might just as well buy it from you as a complete stranger. How will they know you're selling cars if you don't tell them? Word of mouth is the strongest advertising there is, and I'm sure they will tell their friends.

Another way to make contacts in the community is to join organizations. I belong to a number of outdoor and wildlife organizations where I've made many connections and sold cars as a result of those affiliations.

Other places to find referrals could be body shops where they see totaled cars and their customers are looking for new ones. Service stations that are not car dealerships are also great. I used to leave "bird dog" cards at one station, and I can't recall how many times I paid them $50.00 for a referral that ended in a sale. Insurance agents are also great, because people will often call them about rates on a particular car before they even buy the car. I worked with my insurance agent, and sometimes he quoted great car insurance rates to my prospects who were looking for a way to justify a payment schedule. The $10 per month he saved my customer on insurance helped seal the deal. Often the car buyer went to my insurance agent for their car insurance when they found out the better price, and in turn my agent referred new buyers to me as thanks for getting him new insurance customers.

Customer Follow-up Schedule

You'll also want to maintain contact with anyone you've ever sold a car to. Keeping your name in front of them will result in more business for you.

Call them Five times in the first year

- **First Thank You Call:** Between 24-48 hours after the car is delivered. "Thank you! Any problems or questions?"

- **CSI Call:** Approximately 14 days or prior to the manufacturer contact. "Is everything okay? Have you received the CSI Survey?"

- **Referral Call:** 45 days. " $50 Bird Dog fee. Do you happen to know anyone who needs a car?"

- **Anniversary Call:** One year. "Is everything okay, referral?

- **Birthday:** Happy Birthday!

These calls help you remember your customers, what they look like and what they drive. If you see them on the street you can greet them and know something about them. This business becomes very easy when all you deal with is repeats and referrals. If you take the time to follow-up and get interested in your customers' lives the ongoing contact with your previous customer base will ensure your success.

Additional Topics

For those of you not familiar with the internal workings of a car deal, I've prepared some information to help you understand. Upon entering the business, the only perspective that we have in regards to a car deal is one of a consumer. We soon come to find out the dealership looks at it quite differently.

Math

Below is an explanation of how a car deal is calculated along with the terminology used in the process:

MSRP = Window sticker

Invoice = Dealer Cost

MSRP — Invoice = Margin (markup)

MSRP — Selling Price = Discount

Selling Price — Invoice = Gross Profit

A.C.V. = Actual Cash Value (appraised value)

Trade Allowance — A.C.V. = Over allowance

Over-allowance = Discount

Here are some examples to help illustrate the terminology and its practical application:

Example 1 – An Outright Deal

Results

MSRP = $20,000	Margin = $2,500
Invoice = $17,500	Discount = $1,300
Selling Price = $18,700	Gross Profit = $1,200

Example 2 – Trade

Results

MSRP = $21,000	Margin = $2,500
Invoice = $18,500	Discount = $1,000
Trade Allowance = $11,000	Gross Profit = $1,500
A.C.V. = $10,000	

Example 3

To calculate the amount financed in example two,
noting a $5,000 payoff of the loan remaining on the trade-
in, we would use the following formula:

$$
\begin{aligned}
\text{MSRP} &= \$21,000 \\
\text{Trade Allowance} &= \underline{\$11,000}
\end{aligned}
$$

Trade Difference =	$10,000	(taxable amount)
Tax +	650	(6.5%)
License & fees +	350	
Total Due	$11,000	

Balance owing +	$5,000
Amount financed =	$16,000

Leasing

Nine Advantages to Leasing Over Buying

- **Short-term commitment:** 36 months as opposed to 48 or 60.

- **Less up front out of pocket expense:** The start-ups on a lease will typically be less than the down payment required on a purchase.

- **Monthly cash flow:** Payments on the same vehicle are less on a lease than they are on a buy.

- **Less mechanical expense:** Since you're changing vehicles every three years, there are very few miles when you are not under warranty.

- **New car more often:** Every three years.

- **More vehicle for my budget:** You can lease more vehicle for $300 than you can finance for $300 a month.

- **No risk of resale (closed-end lease only):** The customer is never held accountable for the future market value of the vehicle. If the car were worth more than the residual, the customer would want to either buy it or trade it. On the other hand if it were worth less, the customer would want to walk away.

- **Buy a used car for wholesale value or less:** I suggest to the customer that with one month remaining on the lease they should come back to the dealership to get the car appraised. If the market value is equal to or greater than the residual, customers will be paying a wholesale price or less. They are also buying a used car that they are extremely familiar with and have maintained themselves.

- **Gap insurance:** On most leases, the lease company provides the lessee with insurance that covers any potential negative equity in the event of the vehicle being totaled.

Leasing Class

A number of years ago, I came to the conclusion that leasing was going to become more and more popular. Due to the ever-increasing price of vehicles, people would consider alternative forms of financing in order to keep their payments affordable. The first thing I needed to investigate were the reasons why someone would choose *not* to lease. The most common objections that I heard were,

- "I drive too many miles."
- "I want to own it."
- "I can't see making all those payments and ending up with nothing."

Faced with these objections, I designed a presentation that dealt with all of them and explained it in a way that the customer could understand. I felt that the easiest way to do this was to compare a lease to a buy. The presentation started with defining the terminology used in a lease. Explain these terms:

RESIDUAL = the estimated future wholesale value of a vehicle at lease end. It is always calculated as a percentage of MSRP. Every lease company has what they call a "residual value lease guide" and in that guide they estimate the approximate amount of depreciation a vehicle is going to suffer over a given term. If you looked up the vehicle of interest by year, make, model and trim level, you would see something like this.

MSRP = $20,000

%	Residual	
24 MO	68	$13,600
30 MO	63	$12,600
36 MO	58	$11,600

CAPITALIZED COST = the equivalent of amount financed

CAPITALIZED COST REDUCTION = The equivalent of down payment.

START UPS = The sum total of first month's payment + security deposit + license and fees, and in some states tax is also required to be paid up front.

First month's payment	$300
Security deposit	$350
License & Fees	$350
Tax (where applicable)	_____
Total start-ups	$1000

After explaining the terminology to the customer, compare a buy to a lease so they understand the differences.

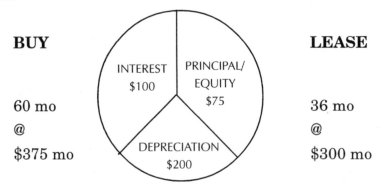

BUY

60 mo

@

$375 mo

LEASE

36 mo

@

$300 mo

Explain that the customer has these two choices. Either buy for a 60-month term with payments of $375/month or lease for a 36-month term with payments of $300/month.

If the customer chooses to buy, each and every time that the customer sends their payment of $375 to the bank, that payment is basically being divided into three different pieces of the pie. The three pieces are interest, principle/equity, and depreciation.

When you lease, you are not contributing to the principal/equity. Leasing is not designed for you to gain equity; it is designed for you to only pay for the part of the vehicle that you are using. There are only two numbers involved in a lease payment, monthly service charge (interest), and monthly depreciation. If the customer initially objected to leasing due to the fact that he or she thought it was a waste of money and stated, "I can't see making all those payments and ending up with nothing," I would explain to him or her why that is not true. If you make the decision to buy and finance for 60 months, a lender, depending upon the customer's credit, would require at least 10% down which in this case would be $2000. If you chose to lease, you are only required to have $1000 out of pocket for your startups. Therefore, you are already $1000 ahead. Additionally, for the next 36 months, $75 per month will be added to the savings. With the $1000 savings up front and the $2700 savings over the next thirty-six month period, the total now comes to $3700 over the term of the lease. Your pie chart illustration would now look like this.

INITIAL SAVINGS	$1000
36 X 75 =	$2700
TOTAL SAVINGS =	$3700

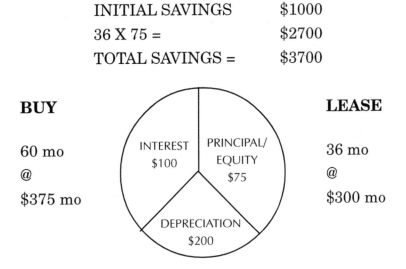

BUY

60 mo

@

$375 mo

INTEREST $100

PRINCIPAL/ EQUITY $75

DEPRECIATION $200

LEASE

36 mo

@

$300 mo

Then I would turn to the customer and ask whether or not he still thought that he ended up with nothing. I'd also ask him if after making 36 payments on a 60-month contract he still thought that he would have $3700 in equity.

For people that thought they drove too many miles to lease, for instance 25,000 miles per year, I would respond as follows:

"Let me explain why leasing may actually be a better option for you." I would then give the customer two choices: Buy for $375 per month, or lease for $300 per month.

"After 36 months of a 60-month finance contract, you will still owe 24 payments of $375. Now you have a 3-year-old vehicle with 75,000 miles on it. What will it be worth in comparison to what you owe? You will probably be in a negative equity situation."

The problem with high mileage drivers is that they often finance for the longest term possible and ultimately never make a big enough payment to get into an equity situation. In other words, the vehicle is depreciating at a faster rate than they are buying the balance down. The end result is that they are terminally "upside down" and always owe more than their vehicle is worth.

Let's go one step further. It's 48 months into a 60-month contract and the customer still has 12 payments left of $375 and owns a 4-year-old, 100,000-mile vehicle.

When will this customer be in an equity situation? When the vehicle is paid off. Now they have a 5-year-old vehicle with 125,000 miles on it. What it is worth? Not much. Additionally, how much mechanical repair expense have they suffered in the last two-years and 50,000 miles?

In the event that a customer drives more than a standard 15,000 miles a year, you should build in the additional miles that are needed. Most lease companies will reduce the residual by .10 a mile. For example, if the customer anticipates needing an additional 10,000 miles, the residual will be reduced by $1,000.

If they don't build in the excess miles, the lease company will charge the customer .15 to .18 per mile. This charge only applies to a customer who makes a decision to "walk away." At the end of the lease the customer has three choices:

- Buy it.
- Trade it.
- Walk away.

The value of this vehicle in 36 months will obviously dictate which choice will be best.

Forms

New Career Letter

Date

Name
Address
City, State, Zip

Dear _____,

I wanted to drop you a quick note to let you know that I have decided to change careers. I have accepted a position at _____ and am very excited about it. In considering a new career, I found that the automobile business and this organization offered all of the things that I was looking for.

I am truly committed to giving my customers a "different experience" while shopping for a vehicle, and if given the opportunity I will expose you to a straight forward, honest, and ethical approach to selling automobiles, with the ultimate goal being a "completely satisfied" customer.

I would also welcome and appreciate any referrals that you could send me for new or used vehicles. If your referral results in a sale, the dealership has authorized me to send you a $ referral fee. Thank you, and I hope to see you soon.

Sincerely,

Delivery Check List

Customer Name: _____

Customer Phone Number: _____

Vehicle Purchased: _____

Date of Delivery:_____ Stock #: _____

- ❏ Explained Owner's Manual
- ❏ Explained Warranty Coverage
- ❏ Explained Maintenance Requirements
- ❏ Familiarized Customer with Service Department
- ❏ Customer was Introduced to Service Personnel
- ❏ Salesperson Demonstrated all Features on Vehicle
- ❏ Customer was given Delivery Checklist
- ❏ Customer was Introduced to Sales Manager
- ❏ Vehicle Interior and Exterior Clean and Undamaged
- ❏ Customer Informed of Customer Survey

_____   _____
CUSTOMER SIGNATURE   SALESPERSON SIGNATURE

Notes:

Gas Mileage Comparison

		OLD		NEW
Miles/Year		_____	.	_____
MPG	÷	_____	÷	_____
Gal/Year	=	_____	=	_____
Cost/Gallon	x	_____	x	_____
$ Gas/Year	=	_____	=	_____
Savings/Year				_____
			÷	12

Savings/Month $ _____

Looking in the Mirror

Being brutally honest, rate yourself (1-10) on the following:

_____	Product Knowledge
_____	Following up Prospects
_____	Following up Customers
_____	Daily Activity Level
_____	Commitment to the Automobile Business

Steps to the Sale:

_____	Meet and Greet
_____	Qualify
_____	Select and Demo
_____	Feature/Benefit
_____	Trade Evaluation
_____	Selling Yourself
_____	Selling the Dealership
_____	Asking for and Getting a Commitment
_____	Overcoming Objections
_____	Negotiate and Close

Self Evaluation

Dates:

	Number	%	Goal	Steps
Ups				
Demos			80%	1, 2, 1/2, 3
Write-ups			60%	1/2, 3, 4, 5, 6
Sold			60%	7

Plan of Action:

Customer Follow-Up Schedule

	When	Call	Topic of Conversation
(daily)	24-48 Hrs	Thank you	Thank you, any questions/ problems?
(daily)	14 Days	C.S.I.	Any questions/problems? Survey.
(daily)	45 Days	Referral	Any questions/problems? Referrals?
(1st wk)	6 Months	Check up	Any questions/problems? Referrals?
(2nd wk)	1 Year	Anniversary	Any questions/problems? Happy Anniversary
(daily)	on Birthday	Birthday	Happy Birthday!

PROSPECT LOG

DATE	PROSPECT NAME	PHONE	VEHICLE/INTEREST	TRADE-IN	D	W/S	L	COMMENTS

Delivery Log

Month: ___ **Year:** ___

Customer	Birthday	Phone	Address	TY	CSI	REF	6	Anniversary	Notes
	1)	H:							
	2)	W:							
	1)	H:							
	2)	W:							
	1)	H:							
	2)	W:							
	1)	H:							
	2)	W:							
	1)	H:							
	2)	W:							

BIRD DOG REQUEST

Enclosed are some of my business cards. If you ever come across a friend, relative, neighbor, or business acquaintance that is in the market for a new or used vehicle, please give them my card. If your referral results in a sale from me, the dealership has authorized me to send you a token of my appreciation. See an example below!

ABC Motors   Date _____
1234 Referral Drive
Thank You, USA

Pay to the order of _____ Amount _____

_____

Memo   Bird Dog   Signature _____

Acknowledgments

Thanks to:

My Mom for her unconditional love, support & belief in me throughout my life.

Don Smith and Joan Olson for their professionalism, expertise and commitment in helping to make this dream become a reality.

Pat Callahan for giving me my first job in sales which ultimately helped me find my call in life.

Mike Allison, who in the beginning, saw enough potential in me to give me the one last chance I needed to succeed.

Tom Kadlec for giving me opportunities at times in my life when others might not have.

Kimberly Grier for her help & support throughout this project. John Jenson for his belief in me.

Jackie B. Cooper & Dick Gardner whose teachings gave me a great deal of my inspiration.

And finally to Tammy, Angie, Michael, and Tyler, my personal inspiration.

ORDER FORM

What You Need to Succeed
Making Car Sales a Career Rather Than a Job
A Straight Forward, Honest, & Ethical Approach to Selling

by Mike "Radar" Radosevich

Share with a Friend or a Colleague

QUANTITY	NUMBER	TITLE	PRICE	TOTAL
	1-886513-68-6	What You Need to Suceed	$24.95	
	Sales Tax (Minnesota Residents) X .065			
	Shipping & Handling		3.25	
		Additional copies .55 each		
	TOTAL			

Name: _____

Address: _____

City: _____ State: _____ Zip: _____

Charge Card ❑ Visa ❑ MasterCard

Card Number: _____

Expiration Date: _____

KIRK HOUSE PUBLISHERS
PO Box 390759
Minneapolis, MN 55439

Fax: 952-835-1828
Toll Free: 1-888-696-1828
Email: publisher@kirkhouse.com